Dr. Seuss

Twayne's United States Authors Series

Children's Literature

Ruth K. MacDonald, Editor

TUSAS 544

DR. SEUSS (TED GEISEL)
(1904–   )
Photograph by Antony Di Gesu.

Dr. Seuss

Ruth K. MacDonald
New Mexico State University

Twayne Publishers • Boston
A Division of G.K. Hall & Co.

Dr. Seuss
Ruth K. MacDonald

Twayne's United States Authors Series
Children's Literature/TUSAS 544

Copyright © 1988 by G.K. Hall & Co.
All rights reserved.
Published by Twayne Publishers
A division of G.K. Hall & Co.
70 Lincoln Street
Boston, Massachusetts 02111

Copyediting supervised by Barbara Sutton
Book production by Janet Zietowski

Typeset in 10/13 Century Schoolbook
by Compset, Inc. of Beverly, Massachusetts

Printed on permanent/durable acid-free paper
and bound in the United States of America

Library of Congress Cataloging-in-Publication Data

MacDonald, Ruth K.
    Dr. Seuss / Ruth K. MacDonald.
        p.   cm.—(Twayne's United States authors series ;
TUSAS 544. Children's literature)
    Bibliography: p.
    Includes index.
    ISBN 0-8057-7524-2
    1. Seuss, Dr.—Criticism and interpretation. 2. Children's
literature, American—History and criticism. I. Title. II. Title:
Doctor Seuss. III. Series: Twayne's United States authors series ;
TUSAS 544. IV. Series: Twayne's United States authors series.
Children's literature.
PS3513.E2Z77   1988
813'.52—dc19   88-16480
                                                          CIP

For David and Jocelyn Shepard

Contents

Preface

This book is the first full-length study of Dr. Seuss and his work. For all his notoriety and success, his work has received little discussion among scholars and critics of children's literature. Though his books are consistently reviewed, the overwhelmingly congratulatory tone of the reviewers has not led to critical evaluation of the author's craft and his accompanying illustration. There have been some article-length studies that give broad overviews. But the in-depth commentary that Seuss's work deserves has not been forthcoming until now.

Popularity can be misleading. Simply because an author is well known and his books widely marketed and purchased does not mean that there is no literary value to his work. Dr. Seuss's works seem verbally simple, but the appearance is deceiving. His books do not come without hard work, craftsmanship, and a thorough grounding in the history of English and American literature. Indeed, they deserve consideration as literature, along with an assessment of their debt to earlier literature and their influence on that which followed. Dr. Seuss first established his reputation in children's-book circles for his illustration; his two Caldecott Honor Books attest to the recognition his artwork gained for him. But it is the quality of his stories that keeps readers coming back, and that led to the original suggestion that he try his hand at the beginner reading book, a form whose simplicity results not from serendipity but rather from skill.

Dr. Seuss's popularity is not simply luck, either, but rather the result of a careful assessment of what children, especially American children, like to read. Above all else, Dr. Seuss has brought pleasure to American children; the citation for his Pulitzer Prize in 1984 particularly commends the entertaining qualities of his books. He succeeds because of his respect for children; because of his willingness to participate with them in their preferred kinds of humor and his willingness to exert himself to tell them an excellent story; and because of his ability to streamline and encourage the reading process for the beginner reader. His books are well received by the older segment of his audience because he manages to impart serious messages parents approve of, without preaching to children. These sources of Seuss's popularity receive focus in this study, as well.

The primary focus throughout this book is on the language of the author; this is, after all, a book in a series on authors. The illustrations obviously deserve commentary, though they are not as extensively treated here as in books about illustration for children. But the felicities of being one's own illustrator demand a consideration of both media together. Since part of the graphic design includes the placement of text on the page, Seuss's attention to typographical conventions is also studied.

Above all, this study seeks to identify underlying themes and patterns over the author's career, and to point to developments in the author's style. Dr. Seuss has frequently been identified as one of the most American of authors and illustrators; a clearer definition of this Americanism is attempted here. His view of childhood, consistent with that of other Americans, receives articulation as well. In the case of the Beginner Books, there is an examination as well of the publisher's marketing techniques to appeal to that American book-buying public. Since Dr. Seuss is president of the Beginner Books division of Random House, he has a hand in shaping the books that appear with the division's logo. His ability to sell books, as well as to market them, is crucial to his longlasting success.

This book is divided into six chapters. The first contains as much biographical information as is available, given the author's flippant answers to the direct questions of reviewers, and his consistent avoidance of the public limelight. The second chapter studies the author's earliest books for children, to establish the state of Dr. Seuss's skills as author-illustrator at the beginning of his career as a children's book creator, and to set forth those themes and techniques that carry through his career. The third chapter studies the major books written after his World War II military service but before the great success of *The Cat in the Hat* and the Beginner Books. Several of these books received awards from professional library associations and established Dr. Seuss as an important figure in children's literature. Chapter 4 examines at length the appeal of *The Cat in the Hat* and the other Beginner Books and Bright and Early Books. Dr. Seuss's philosophy behind these books for beginning readers is also discussed. Attention in this chapter is devoted particularly to *The Cat in the Hat* and its sequels, with lesser attention given to other books in the two series. Chapter 5 deals with Seuss's controversial "message" books, which appeared after his great success with the Beginner Books and which tested his audience's toleration for politics in a medium elsewhere thought to be an inappropriate vehicle for such messages. The last chapter places Dr. Seuss in the context of the tradition of children's literature, and examines the influences on his work, and his influence on other children's writers and illustrators. I have excluded collections of short stories from consideration, since they are simply shorter versions of his achievements in the full-length storybook. I have also not included commentary on his films, since his children's books are clearly his great achievement in life.

Ruth K. MacDonald

New Mexico State University

Acknowledgments

I gratefully acknowledge the assistance of the Arts and Sciences Research Fund of New Mexico State University in providing funding for this project.

Permission to quote from the texts of the following copyrighted works, all by Dr. Seuss, is gratefully acknowledged to Random House, Incorporated: *Horton Hatches the Egg* (1940); *McElligot's Pool* (1947); *If I Ran the Zoo* (1950); *Horton Hears a Who!* (1954); *On beyond Zebra!* (1955); *If I Ran the Circus* (1956); *How the Grinch Stole Christmas!* (1957); *The Cat in the Hat* (1957); *The Cat in the Hat Comes Back* (1958); *The Lorax* (1971); *I Can Read with My Eyes Shut* (1978); *The Butter Battle Book* (1984).

Permission to quote from *And To Think That I Saw It on Mulberry Street* has been granted by the publisher, Vanguard Press, Inc. Copyright © 1937, by Dr. Seuss. Renewed.

Grateful acknowledgment is made to Mr. Jed Mattes of International Creative Management, Inc., New York, agent for Dr. Seuss, for permission to quote from Dr. Seuss's works.

The illustrations are reprinted by arrangement with Random House, Inc., Vanguard Press, Inc., and International Creative Management, Inc.

Chronology

1904	Theodore Seuss Geisel born 2 March in Springfield, Massachusetts, the only son of Theodor and Henrietta (Seuss) Geisel.
1910–1921	Geisel attends Springfield public schools; graduates from Central High School.
1925	A.B. Dartmouth College.
1927	Marries Helen Marion Palmer, 27 November.
1937	*And To Think That I Saw It on Mulberry Street.*
1938	*The Five Hundred Hats of Bartholomew Cubbins.*
1939	*The King's Stilts; The Seven Lady Godivas.*
1940	*Horton Hatches the Egg.*
1943	Serves in U.S. Army Signal Corps and Information and Educational Division under Frank Capra until 1946; receives Legion of Merit for work on informational films.
1946	With Helen Palmer Geisel, *Your Job in Germany (Hitler Lives)*; receives Academy Award for Best Documentary Short Subject.
1947	*McElligot's Pool*, Caldecott Honor Book. With Helen Palmer Geisel, *Design for Death*; receives Academy Award for Best Documentary Feature.
1948	*Thidwick, The Big-Hearted Moose.*
1949	*Bartholomew and the Oobleck*, Caldecott Honor Book.

1950	*If I Ran the Zoo,* Caldecott Honor Book.
1951	*Gerald McBoing-Boing*; receives Academy Award for Best Animated Short Subject.
1953	*Scrambled Eggs Super!*
1954	*Horton Hears a Who!*
1955	*On beyond Zebra!*
1956	*If I Ran the Circus*; honorary doctor of humane letters, Dartmouth College.
1957	Establishes Beginner Books, a division of Random House; *The Cat in the Hat.*
1958	*How the Grinch Stole Christmas! The Cat in the Hat Comes Back.*
1958	*Yertle the Turtle and Other Stories.*
1959	*Happy Birthday to You!*
1960	*One Fish, Two Fish, Red Fish, Blue Fish; Green Eggs and Ham.*
1961	*The Sneetches and Other Stories; Ten Apples up on Top!*
1962	*Dr. Seuss's Sleep Book.*
1963	*Hop on Pop; Dr. Seuss's ABC.*
1965	*Fox in Sox; I Had Trouble in Getting to Solla Sollew; I Wish That I Had Duck Feet.*
1966	*Come Over to My House.*
1967	Death of Helen Palmer Geisel, 23 October.
1968	Marries Audrey Stone Diamond; *The Foot Book; The Eye Book.*
1969	*I Can Lick 30 Tigers Today and Other Stories; Mr. Brown Can Moo! Can You?; My Book about Me by Me, Myself.*

Chronology

1

From Doodles to Doctorates:
The Care and Feeding of a
Picture-Book Author

Dr. Seuss was born Theodore Seuss Geisel, the only child of Theodor Robert and Henrietta Seuss Geisel. Born on 2 March 1904 in Springfield, Massachusetts, the boy was later educated in the Springfield public school system. Though details of his early life are sketchy, two stand out. He reports remembering reading and drawing constantly, beginning his reading career with Dickens and Stevenson. The impulse to doodle appeared as early as the impulse to read, though he never had any art training. The extent of his formal art education was a single drawing lesson in high school, which did not encourage his own style or method of composition. He walked out of the class and never returned.[1] The other detail worth noting is his feeling of shame at his German heritage during World War I. Nicknamed the Kaiser, and sometimes called the Drunken Kaiser, since the senior Geisel was part owner and eventual president of a brewery, Kuhlmbach and Geisel, the boy was occasionally pelted by rocks as he made his way to and from school.[2] From this feeling of social ostracism may derive that need for privacy and avoidance of crowds that now typifies his life.

The one clear influence on his early life was his father; the dedication of two of his most successful books indicates the lasting impression that his father had on him. The dedication of *If I Ran the Circus* reads, "Big Ted . . . the Finest Man I'll ever know"[3]; *McElligot's Pool* is also dedicated to his father. Theodor Robert Geisel worked in his brewery for many years, until he finally became its president, ironically on the same day that Prohibition was declared. Undaunted, he took on the job of superintendent of parks for Springfield, a job that included supervising the local zoo. Much has been made of this possible influence on the future Dr. Seuss, but it is important to note that his father did not become connected with the zoo until Seuss was well into his teens. The many reported visits to the zoo of the young boy are erroneous, and the influence is quite tangential. But Seuss did take one lesson from his father's disappointment as a brewmaster— that perseverance in finding another occupation, and doing it well, is the best way to conduct a life.[4]

In his longtime home on Soledad Hill in La Jolla, California, Dr. Seuss has displayed two mementos from his father. The first is a gift from his father, a plaster casting of a huge dinosaur track found in Springfield. From this huge reminder of an extinct species the son interprets that "he was trying to tell me, in joke form, a species can disappear but still leave a track in the sand,"[5] a sign to the son not only to make something of his life but also to leave something important behind after his death. The second memento is a paper target from a rifle-shooting contest, marked by five bull's-eyes. This is the target that his father shot at to win a world championship in target shooting. Though Dr. Seuss admits that target shooting has no appeal for him, he does emulate his father's perseverance and his quest for perfection. Seuss admits he has never achieved the latter virtue, though his father's example keeps him trying.[6] This restless striving for perfection has led to a life of disciplined writing and drawing, even at a point in life where other successful writers might have slowed down. But Dr. Seuss works an eight-hour day every day, and finds himself ill at ease when he has nothing to do during vacations.

Though Henrietta Geisel's influence is less direct, it is her maiden name her son borrowed as his pseudonym. Although it is pronounced *Soyce* in German, most English speakers pronounce it as it looks, approximating the pronunciation of *Zeus,* the Olympian suggestiveness perhaps influencing the son's choice of names. Seuss began using the pseudonym during his editorship of the Dartmouth College humor magazine. One source claims that the pseudonym became useful when the young collegian was found with a bottle of gin in his dormitory room and was ordered to relinquish the editorship. The pseudonym simply covered up his continued participation in the magazine's publication. But the author himself claims that he used the name for his humorous essays and drawings, saving the name Geisel for the more serious novels he had planned for himself,[7] but which have never materialized beyond an unpublished manuscript of a virtually undecipherable, stream-of-consciousness novel written in his mid-twenties.

Dartmouth and Oxford

After high school, Geisel went to Dartmouth, graduating in 1925. His editorship of and contributions to the college humor magazine, *Jack O'Lantern,* occupied much of his time, since he contributed both cartoons and humorous essays. In later life he has credited his Latin studies in high school and college as influential on his writing, since Latin teaches the derivation of words and, he claims, a respect and love for language. "It allows you to adore words—take them apart and find out where they come from."[8] This analysis of words is characteristic of the author's writing, not only in the extreme consistency with which he uses language in children's books—if something falls down, it must have come from someplace up—but also in his made-up words, which sound like real words because they have linguistic markers, as genuine nouns, verbs, and adjectives do.

He was not an honor student, though he made respectable grades, respectable enough to allow him to apply for a fellowship to Oxford. He told his father of his application for the fellowship, which the father duly reported to the local newspaper as having been awarded to Seuss already. When the son failed to win the fellowship, his father felt forced to send him to Oxford anyway, in order to save face. Geisel went to Oxford in the fall of 1925, with

the avowed purpose of earning a doctorate in literature and becoming a college professor. His notebooks from the lectures he
attended at the time reveal his intentions, for they are filled with
doodles rather than notes, suggesting his increasing frustration
with his studies: "The astonishing irrelevance of graduate work
in English, the committing to memory, for instance of all the
vowel changes in Old English . . . had daunted but not defeated
me."[9] At the end of a year's study, he conferred with his academic
advisor, Emile Legouis, a respected scholar of Jonathan Swift's
work. Legouis suggested that Geisel might research Swift's literary output between ages sixteen and seventeen, to see if he actually wrote anything then. If Geisel discovered something, he
could write his dissertation on it, earn his doctorate, and ensure
his reputation as a literary scholar; if he found nothing, no dissertation, no doctorate, no reputation.

Faced with possible failure after what would be much effort,
and disinclined to pursue his studies anyway, Geisel abandoned
his studies and went on a tour of Europe. Though clearly no
longer an academician, the influence of these studies in English
literature is still clear in Dr. Seuss's work, especially in the early
literary fairy tales *The Five Hundred Hats of Bartholomew Cubbins, The Seven Lady Godivas, The King's Stilts,* and *Bartholomew and the Oobleck,* which all show his familiarity with the
English folk tale. And though memorizing the vowel changes in
Old English may have been tedious, his obvious ability to manip-
ulate the English language has made the author famous and has
proved one of Dr. Seuss's greatest assets.

The one piece of evidence about Geisel's mother from the biog-
raphies is her response to his status as an Oxford dropout: she
"said she was so happy that I would never be a stuffed shirt,"[10] an
unlikely situation, given the son's satiric and irreverent attitude
toward almost everything, revealed in his doodles and essays.

Marriage

The other great influence on his life at the time was his future
wife, Helen Palmer, a fellow student at Oxford, who urged him to

follow his natural inclinations away from academia. Geisel spent the next year roaming around Europe, studying at the Sorbonne and attempting to write the Great American Novel—albeit with long passages in Spanish, a language he did not understand, which led to long, unintelligible passages. After the year, Geisel returned to the United States and married Palmer in November 1927. Throughout his varied career as commercial cartoonist, writer of military films, foreign correspondent, documentary writer, and, finally, children's-book writer, he was encouraged and supported by Palmer, who virtually became his manager, helping him run the Beginner Books division of Random House.

The couple had no children; Dr. Seuss is frequently quoted as saying, "You have 'em, I'll amuse 'em," a flip evasion of questions about his childless state. But he credits his isolation from children of his own for keeping him loyal to his own impulses about what makes a good children's book: "If I had children, I'd have been a failure as an author. I would have sought my children's advice about my manuscripts and they would have told me all sorts of fallacious things. And I would have listened."[11] Like many writers for children, Dr. Seuss claims to write to please himself, a formula that succeeds because of Seuss's recognition of the child in himself.

Geisel and his new wife went to New York after their marriage, where he made a living contributing essays and cartoons to such now extinct weekly and monthly magazines as *PM, Judge, Liberty, Vanity Fair,* and the early *Life*; and to such ongoing magazines as *Redbook* and *Saturday Evening Post*. In these contributions, a sample of which has been collected by Richard Marschall in *The Tough Coughs as He Ploughs the Dough*,[12] the reader finds a racy, even lewd, sense of humor, which one does not associate with the Dr. Seuss of children's books. The viewer also notes an assemblage of made-up beasts, many of whom reappear, some with virtually no alteration, in later Seuss menageries. Above all, the reader is aware of a sensibility that listens carefully to language in its daily use, and pays careful attention to people's foibles and unexamined notions, and to political, if now obscure, events, all of which were grist to be milled and mixed up into Seussian machines, animals, and jokes in his later children's books. In his introduction to the collection, Marschall places Seuss in the humor traditions of S. J. Perelman and Rube Goldberg, in that all are contemporaries, intentionally ridiculous in their humor, and self-deprecating.[13] It was at the end of his magazine contributions, in 1937, in *Judge*, that the "Dr." title was added to Seuss, after having been used with Garibaldi, Theophrastus, and Yogi as pseudonyms for Theodore Geisel. The misappropriation of the degree, Dr. Seuss has quipped, saved his father thousands of dollars.

Geisel continued these contributions through 1937, though in 1928 he became an advertising cartoonist for Standard Oil of New Jersey and originated the promotional campaign for an insecticide called Flit. Standard Oil offered a contract after two cartoons. The most famous is titled "Mediaeval Tenant" and shows a dragon preying on a knight in bed, who quips: "Darn it all, another Dragon. And just after I'd sprayed the whole castle with Flit!" The second Flit cartoon is captioned, "The exterminator-man forgets himself at a flea-circus," and shows the exterminator applying Flit to the circus. After these demonstrations of humor and free advertising, Seuss was hired, for the luxurious salary of $12,000 a year, to continue a series of cartoons featuring Flit as the butt of the joke. The refrain, "Quick, Henry, the Flit!," became a common household phrase. The contract with Standard Oil forbade a number of other commercial ventures that Seuss might have occupied himself with, having found that his work with Flit required only a few days a week. Seuss's lawyer discovered a loophole: the contract did not forbid writing a children's book for publication.

First Children's Books

In 1936, after a particularly rough ocean crossing from France to New York aboard the S.S. *Kungsholm,* Geisel was haunted by the ship's engines and their anapestic rhythm. Instead of trying to forget the noise, he found himself composing a story in verse that would fill out the line, "And to think that I saw it on Mulberry

Street." The boy Marco's tall tale evolved into a story with illustrations, which was subsequently turned down by twenty-seven publishers, since no one was willing to experiment with a book without precedent in the children's book market at the time. An old college friend who had just been appointed children's editor at Vanguard met Geisel on the street in New York and asked him what he had been doing; a glance at the manuscript resulted in a visit to Vanguard's offices and a signed contract for the book within an hour.

The book was well received, and its humor was appreciated even by such austere and venerable critics as Anne Carroll Moore and Beatrix Potter. Geisel followed up with the prose works *The Five Hundred Hats of Bartholomew Cubbins* and *The King's Stilts* in 1938 and 1939, respectively. A single book for adults, *The Seven Lady Godivas,* was published by Vanguard in 1939. The story is about the daughters of Lord Godiva, all of whom are engaged to the Peeping brothers—Peeping Tom, Dick, Harry, Jack, Sylvester, Drexel, and Frelinghuysen. The daughters resolve to learn some horse sense, or horse truths as they call them, before they marry, to avenge the death of their father by a fall from his horse on his way to the Battle of Hastings. Though the ladies are shown naked, the artwork is perhaps more humorous than the story, since Dr. Seuss's limitations as an artist are particularly obvious when he draws the human form. Seuss claims there was a problem with the way he drew their ankles, but one has only to look at their breasts, which are without nipples, to realize that voluptuous erotica was beyond the ability of the artist. The book, probably published on the strength of the sales of his children's books, was a commercial flop, not because it is not funny, but because few people during the Depression had the money to spend on humor.

Army Service and Frank Capra

Geisel continued working on his children's books, publishing *Horton Hatches the Egg* in 1940. He quit his work for Standard Oil in 1941, but was an editorial cartoonist for *PM* magazine from 1940 to 1942, his most notable contribution being his series of anti-Nazi cartoons ridiculing Hitler. In 1943 he began his duty in the Army Signal Corps in Hollywood, making documentaries under the direction of Frank Capra. He advanced to the rank of lieutenant colonel and received the Legion of Merit for his educational and informational films. His most notable contribution to military war films was the "Why We Fight" series of patriotic films.

The influence of Capra on the later works of Dr. Seuss has not been traced, but there are some clear parallels in their works. Obviously, Dr. Seuss's work in film after the war, and his sense of appropriate television adaptation of his books, have their roots in his war experience. Geisel won three Academy Awards after the war: Best Documentary Short Subject in 1946 for *Hitler Lives,* written originally for the army as *Your Job in Germany*; Best Documentary Feature in 1947 for *Design for Death,* written with his wife; and Best Animated Cartoon in 1951 for *Gerald McBoing-Boing.* Obviously Capra's direction of Geisel's talents had tangible payoffs.

But less tangible influences are also clear, especially in the similarities of theme in the works of the two creators. Capra chose to make films about small-town Americans, naifs who face the complexities of situations beyond their control with fortitude and optimism. His belief in the innate goodness of mankind and in the power of the individual to survive and even vanquish larger institutions, and his frank admission of life's inevitable and sometimes devastating complications, are clear in such films as *Mr. Smith Goes to Washington* and *It's a Wonderful Life.* Seuss's subjects have that same naïve strength and optimism, and the constant theme of the good and little overcoming the larger and morally flawed is completely in keeping with Capra's film messages. That typical American faith in common sense and its ability to deflate the pompous and flighty is evident in both men, as is the sense that democracy and uncommon common people are the best government and governors.

La Jolla, California

After the war, Dr. Seuss spent some time in Japan working on *Design for Death* but moved to La Jolla, California, to the abandoned naval observatory that has since been transformed into a home. He created an advertising campaign for Ford while continuing with his children's books. *McElligot's Pool,* the first of three Caldecott Honor Books, so honored for their excellence in children's illustration, was published in 1947. *Thidwick, the Big-Hearted Moose* was published in 1948; *Bartholomew and the Oobleck,* the second of the Caldecott Honor Books, was published in 1949; *If I Ran the Zoo,* the last of the Caldecott Honor Books, was published in 1950. The Caldecott citations indicate a clear recognition of Dr. Seuss's contribution to children's illustration by the Division of Library Services to Children of the American Library Association, the group that gives the Caldecott Medal. But the fact that the books were all Honor Books, all runners-up to the grand prize of Caldecott Medal-winner, may indicate a certain reservation about Dr. Seuss's books. The fact that they are insistently funny, with no grand moral or educational lesson behind them, may have made the books seem less worthy to the judging committee than other books that have not maintained the kind of popularity over the years that the Dr. Seuss books have. The fact that the verse does not aspire to poetry, but is content to be amusing, without any grand pretensions, may also have had some bearing on the committee's selections. None of Dr. Seuss's books has ever won a Newbery Award, honoring the writing, given by the same organization as the Caldecott Medal. Though later awards have recognized the author's contribution to literature as well as illustration, the writing has not received the same level of recognition as the artwork, especially by professionals specializing in children's books.

In spite of this phenomenal record of publication in the years after the war, Geisel still maintained his ties with the filmmaking industry. *Gerald McBoing-Boing* opened the way for *The 5000 Fingers of Dr. T.,* a full-length feature starring Hans Conried, written and designed by Dr. Seuss. Neither film made enough money for Geisel to abandon his publishing. In 1954, Geisel was foreign correspondent for *Life* magazine in Japan, and though his admiration for the Japanese people is clear in his handling of the Whos in *Horton Hears a Who!*, published in 1954, his contributions to the magazine were so ruthlessly edited as to obscure this admiration.

The Cat in the Hat

By 1954, when John Hersey's article on the failures of reading instruction in American schools called upon Dr. Seuss to try his hand at a replacement for the basal reader, Geisel was ready to take on the job. In *On beyond Zebra!*, published in 1955, he ridicules the limitations imposed by traditional school learning, priming the pump for his most famous book, *The Cat in the Hat*, published in 1957, where Dr. Seuss jubilantly breaks the barriers of the basal reader's simplistic language and pedestrian artwork.

It took Geisel over a year to write the book, though he originally thought it might take just a few weeks, given what he remembered about rapidly turning out film scripts during the war. But finding a story and then telling it, using the vocabulary list for beginner books supplied by Houghton Mifflin, proved more difficult than he thought. The book was finally published simultaneously as a textbook by Houghton Mifflin and as a trade book by Random House.

It was a huge success, not only because of its strong story and characterization, but also because it could be published cheaply while still maintaining the quality of the artwork. An improvement in the technique of offset lithography permitted mass merchandising of the book. Without this success, Dr. Seuss would have remained a minor light in the history of children's books. The success prompted Bennett Cerf, then editor at Random House, to claim that Dr. Seuss was the only real genius published on his list, though at the time that list included John O'Hara and William Faulkner.[14]

The Cat in the Hat led to the establishment of the Beginner Books division of Random House, of which Geisel has been president since its inception. Geisel, with much help from his wife, helped to develop the list of picture books suitable for beginning readers. These books do not adhere so strictly to vocabulary lists as does *The Cat,* but still contain simple sentences, and close connection between text and illustration, with nothing in the text that is not in the pictures. The list now features forty-two Dr. Seuss books; eleven Theo. LeSieg books, another Geisel pseudonym, the last name being *Geisel* spelled backward; and one book by Geisel under the pseudonym Rosetta Stone. The market for books for even younger children, with even shorter texts, shorter sentences, and more simplified illustrations, led to the Bright and Early series of books, begun in 1968, which also features Seuss and LeSieg titles.

The storybooks continued simultaneously with the Beginner Books, though there are few remarkable titles from the beginning of the Beginner Books until 1971, with the publication of *The Lorax.* The intense pressure to produce, combined with the guaranteed sales of any Dr. Seuss titles, may explain the lack of interest in the stories and the mechanical quality of the drawings. Some of the books are clearly marketing gimmicks, such as the storybook *Happy Birthday to You!,* the appropriate Dr. Seuss book for any child's birthday, and *The Cat in the Hat Song Book,* a watered-down spin-off riding the success of the first *Cat in the Hat* book. Though the quality of the books may have slacked off, still five of them have made it to the top of the list of children's best-sellers from 1895 to 1975, all of them Beginner Books from 1957 to 1963: *Green Eggs and Ham* (1960) is at the top of the list, followed by *One Fish, Two Fish, Red Fish, Blue Fish* (1960), *Hop on Pop* (1963), *Dr. Seuss's ABC* (1963), and *The Cat in the Hat* (1957). *The Cat in the Hat Comes Back* (1958) is eighth on the list, after formidable competition from E. B. White's *Charlotte's Web* and L. Frank Baum's *The Wonderful Wizard of Oz.* None of

the other Beginner Books appears on the list, nor do any other
Dr. Seuss books.[15] Obviously, some of the credit for the books that
do appear is due to the mass marketing of the books, but their
quality cannot be overlooked either.

Later Storybooks

Though in *Yertle the Turtle and Other Stories* (1958) and *The
Sneetches and Other Stories* (1961) both deal with political issues—the former nazism, the latter racism—by the time Dr.
Seuss dealt with them, the issues were considerably less sensitive. The stories were lost amidst the critical attention devoted to
the Beginner Books of the period, and Dr. Seuss became more
associated with these interesting and enjoyable reading books
and less associated with the political books typical of his earlier
career. *The Lorax* (1971) violated the expectations of those familiar with Seuss's Beginner Books, since it is a frank morality tale
about pollution—its sources, its consequences, and the actions
that must be taken to prevent it or undo it. The book was made
into a television special and received the Critics Award at the
International Animated Cartoon Festival in Zagreb, Yugoslavia,
and the Silver Medal from the International Film and TV Festival
of New York.

Kudos

Though the Beginner Books might not all have been of the quality
of Dr. Seuss's other books, they made the public increasingly
aware of the author's achievements as a writer. Dartmouth's
granting of an honorary doctor of humane letters degree in 1956
made an "honest man" out of the author, who had earlier simply
appropriated the title. This was the first in a long line of degrees
honoring a lifetime of contribution to children's literature. Honorary doctorates followed from American International College in
Springfield, Massachusetts, in 1968; Lake Forest College, Illinois,

in 1977; Whittier College, California, in 1980; J. F. Kennedy University, Orinda, California, in 1983; Princeton University, in 1985; and the University of Hartford, Connecticut, in 1986. Seuss also received the Roger Revelle Award, equivalent to an honorary doctorate, from the University of California, San Diego, in 1978. The degrees from Whittier and Kennedy were doctor of literature degrees, indicating a particular appreciation for Dr. Seuss's accomplishments in verse; the degree from Princeton, a doctor of fine arts, honors his illustration with the distinction of a degree.

Other honors followed, including Dr. Seuss Day, proclaimed by the governors of Alabama, Arkansas, California, Delaware, Georgia, Kansas, Minnesota, and Utah, to celebrate his seventy-seventh birthday on 2 March 1981. The Laura Ingalls Wilder Award from the Association for Library Service to Children of the American Library Association honored Dr. Seuss in 1980 for "lasting and substantial contribution to children's literature," perhaps in lieu of all the Newbery awards he did not receive from this same organization. The Regina Medal from the Catholic Library Association in 1982 honors his books for the simple criterion of "excellence." Also in this year followed a Special Award for Distinguished Service to Children from the National Association of Elementary School Principals. Along the way to collecting all these awards Dr. Seuss also received the first Outstanding California Author Award from the California Association of Teachers of English in 1976, a Peabody Award for his television specials "How the Grinch Stole Christmas" and "Horton Hears a Who" in 1971, Emmy Awards in 1977 for "Halloween is Grinch Night" and 1982 for "The Grinch Grinches the Cat in the Hat," and finally, a Pulitzer Prize in 1984 "for his contribution over nearly half a century to the education and enjoyment of America's children and their parents." The attention these awards brought to the normally reclusive author has made him uncomfortable, though not so much so that he was scared away from a birthday celebration in 1986 in New York to celebrate the release of his adult book *You're Only Old Once! A Book for Obsolete Children.*

Not all the attention has been positive. With the publication of *The Butter Battle Book* in 1984, which took on the issue of imminent nuclear disaster, critics charged Dr. Seuss with a number of heinous crimes against childhood: oversimplifying the issue; frightening children; introducing them to subject matter they did not need to know about until they were older; villifying the effectiveness of nuclear deterrence; and frustrating children with the open, unresolved ending. In spite of the response of the critics, the book made the juvenile best-seller list in the *New York Times* and praise from many groups, especially nuclear disarmament activists.

The death of Helen Palmer Geisel in 1967, Geisel's remarriage to Audrey Stone Diamond in 1968, advancing age, and his sometimes precarious health—a heart attack, cancer surgery, and cataract surgery—have at times slowed the author's production of new books. But he remains active as president of Beginner Books and has plans for a number of new projects, such as Broadway musicals, new Beginner Books, and some video adaptations of his characters and stories to be used in educational software by Coleco. He works eight hours every day, ignoring any suggestions that he retire, working on two or three projects at a time. He remains a voracious reader, which may be one reason he keeps working and reworking his verse, so that it will measure up to the other examples of literature he reads; he admits to being unable to write in prose anymore. Though sometimes condemned in his later years for his moralizing, he says that the morals sometimes make their way into the stories as a result of the subject matter; he is never blatant, except perhaps in his political books. By his own count, there are only six "message books" out of forty-two,[16] which proves, he claims, that he is not really as overwhelmingly moralistic as critics have made him out to be.

He has never improved his drawing, but then he admits that he really cannot draw; so he simply capitalizes on his incapacity. "I've taken the awkwardness and peculiarities of my natural style and developed them."[17] His style has become internationally recognizable; even without the Cat in the Hat logo on the cover of the Beginner Books, even very young children can recognize his two-dimensional style, with its loud, even garish, colors and thick, bold lines. One critic has claimed a family similarity among his characters, based on two features: "slightly batty, oval eyes and a smile you might find on the Mona Lisa after her first martini."[18] His books reach an international audience because of their translation into such diverse languages as Polish and Maori, though the author maintains a particular fondness for those printed in braille. In spite of this international readership, the books remain particularly American: bright, even brash; optimistic, convinced of children's abilities to read and to reason; and encouraging of self-confidence, imagination, and appreciation of others.

2

The Early Books

Mulberry Street and the other books that followed and were published by Vanguard Press show Dr. Seuss beginning to work out his preposterous stories by making them more preposterous. They also show his menagerie of animal characters and peculiar wide-eyed humans who filled his books for children over the following decades. His drawing style has not really evolved from the bold lines and loud colors of these early books, although his adequate ability to lay out a page in a way that entertains without confusing a child with its detail becomes more skillful over time. Seuss's ability to design a page in order to invite a child to read on is evident in these books, though here, too, he improves with time. But his ability to tell a good story is the key ingredient here, one that is evident from the beginning.

And the key to a good children's picture book is a good story—one with clear forward movement, spareness of description, and rapid, unequivocal resolution of the issues. Poetry, especially the anapestic tetrameter characteristic of Seuss's books, helps this movement by carrying the reader forward, helping to predict the pronunciation of words and encouraging progress through the text. Seuss's verse is particularly unpoetic in its lack of poetic devices, but the spareness of style frequently camouflages an unexpected complexity of narrative technique, all designed to help the child reader master the text.

Seuss's usual design for a story is cumulative, with details continually added to a core story, which is initially quite spare. These details are added both verbally and visually. In the genre of the picture book, the pictures are an integral part of the "reading" of the story—one reads both text and picture, each helping to interpret the other. A strong figure on a simple background helps the interpretation by focusing clearly on the important details as they are added. The turning of the page, the brevity of the text per page, the pause to view the picture before the page turn, all give a feeling of rapid pacing and satisfactory progress through the book. There are certain conventions to be mastered in "reading" the pictures—the child must learn that the text, though it occupies space on the page, is not part of the picture; the lines emanating from the figure may indicate movement or emotion; the person on an earlier page is the same person on the next, not a twin to the earlier character. Individual pages are meant to be viewed as part of a succession rather than as individual works of art, like those hung in museums. Thus, they are not static but, again, are full of movement. The child reader's experience depends on the success of both the language and the illustration; the experience cannot be captured in a single medium.

Even in these early books Dr. Seuss shows his intuitive grasp of the expectations of the child reader and the possibilities, as well as the limitations, of the picture book story and illustration.

And To Think That I Saw It on Mulberry Street

The anapestic rhythm that has become the trademark of Seuss's verse for children was inspired by the constant droaning engine he heard during an ocean voyage. The refrain in the book, "And that is a story that no one can beat / And to think that I saw it on Mulberry Street,"[1] kept repeating itself in Seuss's mind during the trip, and challenged him to come up with such an unbeatable tale. Mulberry Street is part of Seuss's native Springfield, Massachusetts, and Marco, the main character, was a real boy, to whose mother the story is dedicated. But the "story that no one can beat" is pure imagination, the product of a little boy's trying to please his father by being able to give some good account of what he saw coming home from school. It is also the result of Seuss's relentless challenging of himself to come up with an unbeatable story, one that he can consistently top with yet another unbeatable story—by embellishing the details.

The tall tale starts with Marco designing a story to tell his father about what he has seen. The tale begins with a horse-drawn cart and gradually grows to a circus-wagon carrying a brass band, the wagon drawn by two giraffes and a blue elephant with a rajah on his back, accompanied in the back by a trailer with a man listening to the band, all led by a police escort of motorcycles. This troop is showered with confetti by a flying ace, and is greeted by the mayor and all the aldermen in town. Even this long list of embellishments does not cover all the changes that the boy makes while making the tale bigger and better, including his final addition of a Chinese man, a magician, and a man with a long beard. When he finally gets home, he is so overcome by the elegant detail that he hardly knows where to start when his father asks him what he's seen, and so deflated, he answers that he has seen "Nothing . . . / But a plain horse and wagon on Mulberry Street," returning to reality with a resounding thud.

Marco's father asks him every day what he has seen, just as many children are asked daily what they learned in school. But the father's motivation is unclear: on the one hand he wants to be told about something interesting, which would presumably indicate the boy's superior powers of observation. But on the other hand, the father wants the truth. Given that the boy's route is a path prosaic enough to be called Mulberry Street, and his destination is as ordinary as home or school, it is not always possible for him to find something of interest. So he resorts to embellishment, in the tradition of the tall tale in the United States, where everything is bigger and better, including the stories. Once the story gets started, Marco continues adding to it, to improve it and make it more impressive, so that it truly becomes unbeatable even while it becomes more unbelievable. In an effort to bolster his self-confidence in answering his father, he keeps adding to the story to make it more elegant, stylish, and worthy of his father's interest and, therefore, his approval, both of Marco and of his story. The story seems to succeed as Marco approaches the end of his journey home and the end of his accumulation of details. But at the last moment, his father's presence deflates both boy and story, reasserting truthfulness and reality, but still not destroying the rollicking raucousness of the story that has just been bodied forth, both in words and pictures.

Seuss related in a magazine interview the four main reasons for the other publishers' rejection of the book:

1. Fantasy doesn't sell.
2. Verse doesn't sell.
3. It had no "pattern" (a term even Seuss did not explain).
4. It wasn't "practical"—that is, it didn't teach the child how to become a better child, or grown-up, or mortician.[2]

In spite of these objections, Seuss and Vanguard managed to make a success of the story and launch Seuss's career as a writer for children.

Marco is the prototype for a number of other boys in Seuss's later books—Bartholomew Cubbins of *The Five Hundred Hats* and *Bartholomew and the Oobleck,* Gerald McGrew of *If I Ran the Zoo* and Morris McGurk of *If I Ran the Circus.* Marco even reappears in *McElligot's Pool* with another imaginary tale of increasingly unlikely detail. Unlike Bartholomew, though, these other boys, including Marco, are capable of remarkable imaginative powers, starting with the most pedestrian of details and building, through cumulative embellishments, as Tom Sawyer does with his games, to the most gorgeous, preposterous finishes. Like most American children since the landing of the Pilgrims, Marco is supposed to think for himself and answer truthfully, speaking his own mind, when he is spoken to. Marco's father sees the walk to and from school as an experience as worthy of recounting as the actual school day. As Marco says in opening the story,

> When I leave home to walk to school,
> Dad always says to me,

"Marco, keep your eyelids up
And see what you can see."

The complication comes from the discrepancy between what Marco thinks he has seen, a clear indication that his credibility is in question, and what his father thinks of his stories: "Your eyesight's much too keen. / Stop telling such outlandish tales. Stop turning minnows into whales." But it is this ability to turn the small into the large that marks Marco's story as wonderful and entertaining. And it is his father's insistence that there be something unusual everyday that makes Marco resort to these stories; as father says at the end of the story, just as Marco stands tongue-tied, reconsidering the wisdom of telling his amazing story, "Was there nothing to look at . . . no people to greet? / Did *nothing* excite you or make your heart beat?" Clearly, father is begging for an extraordinary story, something beyond "a horse and a wagon." Hence, Marco's wish to present himself as a keen observer and outstanding storyteller, to tell the "story that no one can beat."

Marco's tale depends on its cumulative structure, starting with the bare facts and adding progressively unlikely details. Though the story has internal consistency, it increasingly strays from the actual toward the implausible. The story begins with Marco claiming that he has observed as carefully as possible but has found nothing besides his own feet and the horse and the wagon. He immediately recognizes the inadequacy of this account if presented to his father. "That's nothing to tell of, / That won't do, of course . . ." He then recognizes the potential of these items for a story, realizing that the horse and wagon are "only a *start*." He changes the horse to a zebra, something more unusual. The corresponding picture shows the zebra and wagon as much larger than the horse and wagon, with more motion, and with a more alert look on the faces of both the zebra and the man driving the wagon. The man has acquired a whip, which he smartly brandishes, and with which he urges on the zebra. Even the three potted plants in the wagon, unmentioned details that in the first picture make the wagon seem stable and static, are shown in the second picture jolting and jumping from the swift pace of the wagon. And though Marco concludes that the addition of the zebra makes "a story that no one can beat," yet it is the presence of the zebra that urges him on to embellish even further. Illustration thus underscores the increasing detail and pace of the story—and of Marco's imagination, as he continues to devise the story.

Marco then decides that the zebra deserves a more wonderful vehicle, the cart being "so tame." The wildness of Marco's particular brand of invention becomes clear in his evaluation of his imaginative progress thus far. Marco is also aware that, though his tale appears to the reader and to himself in a visual mode, through the illustrations, his story will eventually be told and will depend on an oral rendition; based on this criterion, he decides to change the driver to a charioteer and, of course, the wagon to a gold and blue chariot, "rumbling like thunder down Mulberry Street!" The sound effects and exotic tinge to the word *charioteer* will make the story all the better in the telling. That the chariot is *"something* to meet" is an indication of Marco's motivation for telling such a story—so that he will feel like something himself, full of confidence and importance, when he finally tells it to his father.

The next step in the developing story is the decision to change the zebra, which Marco judges to be "too small," to a reindeer, which is quicker. The reindeer is also larger—at least partly because of his magnificent rack of antlers, which takes up considerable space on the page and nearly overpowers the small chariot—and "smart," indicating Marco's desire for style and elegance in his story. Though the charioteer still brandishes the whip that the driver had earlier, it is clear that the reindeer has taken control of the ride. While an earlier picture of the zebra begins to intrude from the right page to the left, in the next picture, the reindeer's clouds of dust from his swift movement extend nearly the whole distance across the two pages. Thus, though the picture is similar to the earlier one, it also shows the changes that have occurred in the story, changes not only of detail but also of quality. The story has become more animated, and the details of

Marco's story are beginning to fill up the visual as well as the narrative field.

Marco's need for elegance in the story is clear from the next change he makes, from a chariot with a single charioteer to a sled with two Eskimo, though the picture of the Eskimo retains the detail of the charioteer's boldly flying belt and headband in the second Eskimo's fluttering scarf. Marco makes the change to the sled because it is consistent with the reindeer, and so will make the reindeer "happier," since, according to Marco, reindeer dislike the feel of pulling wheeled vehicles. But Marco also makes the change because the sled is larger and "fancy," and because, as is clear in the illustration, the ride in the sled is much bumpier and full of motion than that in the wheeled chariot.

But the consistency of the reindeer pulling a sleigh seems much too ordinary on second thought to Marco: "Say—*any*one could think of *that,* / Jack or Fred or Joe or Nat—/ Say, even Jane could think of *that.*" Some feminists have balked at the last line, which they interpret as being a slight to the power of female imagination. But Marco's special concern that his story is inadequate is not because even a girl could have imagined it. The boys' names, like Jane's, are ordinary and monosyllabic, as ordinary as one might suppose those children's imaginations are. The insult here is to all other children, not just to girls.

Once again, to improve his story, Marco makes a change—from a reindeer to a blue elephant with a rajah sitting in a howdah on his back. In this alteration, Marco abandons consistency in the story as a concern. In fact, the inconsistency of an elephant with a sleigh and Eskimo makes this change particularly attractive. That the elephant is blue—rather than ordinary gray, or even clichéd pink—makes the change even more vivid. The elephant's gaze, meeting the viewer's, further emphasizes the "fun in his eyes" that Marco imagines for him. His "power and size" are obvious not only from his proportions on the page, but also from the force with which he draws the sleigh, which now hardly touches the ground, and which threatens to throw off the Eskimo riders. The rajah, who is added to give the elephant "a little more tone," is complacently superior, not noticing the world around him, but sitting with utmost disdain, high above the elephant's back, the howdah exaggerating this height even further. His disdain, like his rubies, adds to the "tone" of Marco's story, just as the reindeer makes the story "smart" and chic.

But the lightness of the sleigh bothers Marco, so he changes it to a circus wagon with a brass band, which he describes as both "great" and "big" and implies that it is noisy. In fact, the picture shows that the wagon has a driver and six musicians and includes a calliope, which add to the visual complexity of the story, even though those details are not mentioned in the narrative. That the elephant not only looks but feels "simply grand" is evident from his changed expression, now mimicking the rajah's closed-eyed smugness.

But Marco realizes that the band's effectiveness in his story is limited by its lack of audience, so he adds a trailer onto the back of the circus wagon, with a man to listen to the band. What Marco does not describe, though the picture makes quite obvious, is that this is no simple cart, but a four-wheeled affair, with a stovepipe from which emanates smoke, further filling up the page, and shutters open to reveal a plant in the window. Like a little home, the trailer trails on the left side of the left page, filling up what little space remains horizontally. That the trailer adds extra weight makes Marco question the fairness of the elephant towing the assemblage by himself. So he adds "some helpers. He needs two, at least." What the text neglects to mention is that the helpers are giraffes, who tower above the elephant on either side, with the same smug, superior look as the rajah, being as full of "tone" as he is. The companions clearly delight the elephant, who once again looks at the viewer with "fun in his eyes."

But with this long assemblage, Marco begins to entertain practical considerations, and with a mixture of anxiety and desire, contemplates an upcoming intersection on Mulberry Street:

> But now what worries me is this. .
> Mulberry Street runs into Bliss,
> Unless there's something I can fix up,
> There'll be an *awful* traffic mix-up!

The possibility of collision, with its disorganization, noteworthy detail, and noise, would further enhance the tale, but might also stop it dead in its tracks. So Marco introduces a three-police escort on motorcycle, "with Sergeant Mulvaney, himself, in the lead," the phrase indicating not only the importance of the people being escorted, since the sergeant leads the parade, but also the Irish heritage of "himself," Sergeant Mulvaney. Even the rajah and the giraffes take notice, and the smug expression of smartness is transferred to the policemen, while everyone else in Marco's parade looks on.

The police salute the mayor and the aldermen in their reviewing stand, which this parade then passes on Mulberry Street. Though the mayor now takes on the look of "tone," patronizingly doffing his top hat, the aldermen are less reserved, "All waving big banners / Of red, white and blue," in good patriotic American form. The band's musicians are shown concentrating on their music, as is the practice of bands who wish to show off in front of the reviewing stand. But other members of the procession, the rajah, and the giraffes look round at the mayor, and the rajah even offers an open-handed salute. To top off the parade, Marco adds a passing airplane with daredevils dumping confetti on the procession, which even the sergeant and the rajah look at with expressions of admiration and awe. Only the mayor and the flying ace can maintain expressions of detached, superior dignity. The addition of the airplane and confetti "makes a story that's really not bad! / But it still could be better." But there is hardly any room left on the page or in Marco's imagination, or time left, before Marco arrives home, so he adds—at the bottom of the page, in order to enhance the strangeness of the story,

> . . . A Chinese man
> Who eats with sticks. . . .
> A big Magician
> Doing tricks . . .
> A ten-foot beard
> That needs a comb. . . .
> No time for more,
> I'm almost home.

By this final two-page spread, nearly everyone is cheering and waving, with the confetti pouring down and the dust of the procession and exhaust of the motorcade further adding to the chaos and high spirits. It is no wonder that, when the reader turns the page, and Marco rushes up the stairs to his home, he proclaims: "I felt simply GREAT! / FOR I HAD A STORY THAT NO ONE COULD BEAT! / AND TO THINK THAT I SAW IT ON MULBERRY STREET!"

But his father's greeting deflates his good feelings, and calms his excitement to the point that he cannot think of what to say:

> But Dad said quite calmly,
> "Just draw up your stool
> And tell me the sights
> On the way home from school."

The father's lack of participation in Marco's exuberant feelings draws the boy up short; the feelings are not strong enough to exist without the father's encouragement of them. When Marco fails to respond immediately, his father becomes annoyed, and further undermines the self-confidence with which Marco had entered the house:

> Dad looked at me sharply and pulled at his chin.
> He frowned at me sternly from there in his seat,
> "Was there nothing to look at . . . no people to greet?
> Did *nothing* excite you or make your heart beat?"

Once again, the father demands a good tale, but when Marco needs the time to catch his breath and organize his thoughts, the father misinterprets his son's hesitation, and forces Marco to revise his story. The reader knows that Marco did see people and did find things to look at, was excited, and had a beating heart, at least in his imagination. But the father's calmness so interrupts the boy's mood that all that he can respond is, "Nothing . . . / But a plain horse and wagon on Mulberry Street," the reply accompanied by the same ordinary, uninspired, actionless, picture that first started his fantasy. The fact that his reply is accompa-

. . . A Chinese man
Who eats with sticks. . . .

A big Magician
Doing tricks . . .

A ten-foot beard
That needs a comb. . . .

No time for more,
I'm almost home.

nied by a clear reaction from the boy, "growing red as a beet," indicates Marco's feeling of humiliation—though it is not clear whether he feels bad because he cannot tell his story, or because his fantasy has so far run away with him.

It is possible that Marco has been too busy fabricating his story to notice all the real things on Mulberry Street that might have otherwise caught his attention; but more likely, given Seuss's respect for the power of fantasy and of a good story, he is simply finding a way to amuse himself, and a good way at that. Elsewhere, Michael Steig has commented on what he perceives as Seuss's supression and condemnation of the imagination in *I Wish That I Had Duck Feet* (1965). In that story, a boy contemplates various changes in his body which might make him more interesting and more powerful, but in the end decides that the changes would be impractical or undesirable, and so decides to be his plain self. Like Marco, this boy is capable of the same wild flights of fantasy, and like Marco, in the end abandons them in favor of the literal, if plain, truth. Steig finds this ending oppressive and critical of the value of imagination.[3]

But the visual interest of the stories, and the attention and pleasure that they elicit from the reader, undercut this condemnation. In fact, Seuss celebrates the power of the imagination and provides a safe forum for children to exercise it: in the pages of books. He also eases the child reader back into reality, with the endings of the stories clearly including adults and what happens when older people collide with children's flights of fantasy. But the two books both preserve and perpetuate the stories, and the endings do nothing to undercut the power and pleasure of the imaginations that developed them.

The Five Hundred Hats of Bartholomew Cubbins

Though Dr. Seuss is renowned for his verse, he was also a master of prose, as is seen in *The Five Hundred Hats of Bartholomew Cubbins*. Whereas *Mulberry Street* established his usual verse form, anapestic tetrameter, in this second book, Seuss shows his mastery of the prose form of the literary fairy tale. His work for national magazines, his early attempt at a novel were all in prose, and through this particular piece of fiction, Seuss shows his training, both at Dartmouth and at Oxford, in the history of English language and literature. For *Bartholomew* is a fairy tale in the old English tradition, much like "Jack and the Beanstalk," but with the American element of *The Wizard of Oz.*

The story of the young boy with the magical, although seemingly ordinary, hat opens like the book of Genesis—"In the beginning"[4] evoking the feeling of the older literature on which literary fairy tales depend. And like this old literature is Bartholomew Cubbins's hat. "It was an old one that had belonged to his father and his father's father before him. It was probably the oldest and the plainest hat in the whole Kingdom of Didd." It is a historical hat, existing almost outside of time. But though the hat is plain, like Bartholomew and his ancestors, both hat and descendant stand up well against any other heritage in the story, including that of Nadd, the wise man, who "knows about everything in all my kingdom"; the father of Nadd, who "knows about everything in all my kingdom and in all the world beyond"; and the father of the father of Nadd, who "knows about everything in all my kingdom, in all the world beyond, and in all other worlds that may happen to be." None of these wise men, symbols though they are of the wisdom of the kingdom of Didd, and equipped with beards that are longer with each increasing generation, can figure out the magic of Bartholomew's hat, which refuses to come off his head, even though he obediently removes it when the king comes by. Even the king, who has his own heritage and hat, is confounded and swears "by the Crown of my Fathers!" But though this hat is invested with all the greatness of the kings of Didd, still the hat of Bartholomew and his fathers confounds everyone in the kingdom and gets their attention, as he removes hat after hat, facing all sorts of royal scrutiny and even death for his failure to show reverence for the king and the royal hat by doffing his plain one.

But the title predicts the outcome: Bartholomew has five hundred hats to remove before his king, and though the hats are plain, they have a remarkable persistence. The counting of these hats as he removes them is the task of Sir Alaric, keeper of the king's records and mathematically precise recorder of Bartholomew's hats. The tension in the story mounts as the wise men fail to analyze the mystery of the hats; as the royal magicians can do no better than a spell that will take ten years to work; as the executioner cannot do his job on Bartholomew because, according to the rules of the kingdom of Didd, no one can be executed with his hat on; and as neither the bratty young Grand Duke Wilfred nor the Yeoman of the Bowman can shoot the hat off permanently. The final stroke of tension begins as Bartholomew, led by the king and the young duke, and followed by Sir Alaric, ascends the stairs of the highest turret, so that the king can resort to the final solution: pushing off both the hat and Bartholomew to their ultimate ends. But Sir Alaric has paid careful attention to the number of hats. Though Bartholomew has commenced to removing them frantically, in a last minute effort to save himself, at hat number 451, they begin to change, with the addition of first one, then two, feathers, then jewels and increasingly fancy hatbands, until hat number 500 is grander than the king's crown, and inspires the king's offer of five hundred gold pieces. This hat "had a ruby larger than any the King himself had ever owned. It had ostrich plumes, and cockatoo plumes, and mockingbird plumes, and paradise plumes. Beside *such* a hat even the King's Crown seemed like nothing." In fact, after the king buys it, he puts it on, right over the crown, hiding the crown completely with the last of Bartholomew's hats.

The final hat enshrines Bartholomew forever in the history of the kingdom of Didd, for the king orders that all five hundred hats go on display, "to be kept forever in a great crystal case by the side of his throne." And though the five hundredth hat is preposterously gorgeous, towering like a gaudy peacock on the king's head and totally hiding the royal crown beneath it, yet it suits the king's sense of pride. In contrast, Bartholomew is shown walking bareheaded and comfortable, arm-and-arm with the king, both overshadowed by the ultimate headgear. The king is equally enshrined in the history of the kingdom, for the story is as much his as it is Bartholomew's, which probably has not escaped the royal sense of pride. But Bartholomew's return to his parents' small but cozy home, with the moon shining behind it like a halo, is the final scene in the book. After all, it is his magic, not the king's inept dealings with the hats, that is most memorable.

The magic of the plain, old hat goes down in history, unexplained. No one "could ever explain how the strange thing had happened. They only could say it just 'happened to happen' and was not very likely to happen again." Neither Bartholomew nor the hat is extraordinary, nor even important, as the story begins; both are just loyal subjects of the king who set out in the story with no extraordinary purpose. But the hat is distinguished by its single feather, which sticks up straight in the air, and marks both the hat and the wearer for attention. In fact, the feather particularly recommends the hat to Bartholomew. "But Bartholomew liked it—especially because of the feather that always pointed straight up in the air." No one else in the story has such a prominent feather, though there are clearly more elegant examples of headgear, especially that of the young grand duke, whose hat, like Bartholomew's, is shaped like Robin Hood's simple hunting hat, but has two feathers, both of which are sinuously long, though neither of which stands up straight, as Bartholomew's does.

The red color of Bartholomew's hat further sets him off for attention, for the red of the hat is the only color on any of the pages. Though the narrative does not say so, it seems likely that Bartholomew is easily picked out in the crowd not only by the high feather, which protrudes above the heads of the adults, but also by his possession of color, which sets him out from the black, white, and gray tones everywhere else. One can suppose that a boy who likes his prominent feather also likes the boldness of the red hat. Both feather and color mark the hat like many other magical, important elements in a fairy tale—clearly defined, bold in outline, valuable, at least at first to Bartholomew and later to the king, and prominent. The hat, like the illumination of a capital letter in a medieval manuscript, is the only illustration on the opening page of the story, and stands out from the beginning, indicating its symbolic value as surely as does the title of the story.

The story proceeds by opposites and contrasts. Bartholomew's red feather against the black and white background; the plainness of his first hat compared to the elegance of the crown and the plainness of the crown compared to Bartholomew's five hundredth hat; the king's and the grand duke's temper in contrast to Bartholomew's polite obedience. The opening vantage points of the king and his subject Bartholomew set up this opposition. Bartholomew is not visible to King Derwin in his castle. From his vantage point high in the palace on a mountain, he looks down on his whole kingdom, feeling his importance by his distance: "It was a mighty view and it made King Derwin feel mighty important." In the picture of him looking down on his kingdom, his nose, which is shown to be crooked and unpleasant elsewhere, is here held high in the air as his back faces the viewer. Even the palace guard, who faces the viewer and holds a huge lance guarding the king, holds his nose in the air, a picture that helps, along with the text, to underscore the viewer's perception of King Derwin. The king may be mighty, but he is also mighty arrogant and mighty aloof from his subjects, whose homes stretch out to the horizon of the picture.

From the opposite vantage point, from the smallest dot on the horizon, Bartholomew enjoys the obverse view: up toward the palace, but from his less advantageous viewpoint "far off in the fields." The fact that this is a reversal of positions is made clear by the narrator—"It was exactly the same view that King Derwin saw from his balcony, but Bartholomew saw it backward"—as is the effect of the view on Bartholomew: "It was a mighty view, but it made Bartholomew Cubbins feel mighty small." But Bartholomew's hat, red with a prominent feather, makes him stand out in this picture, and focuses the viewer's attention less on the king's height and more on Bartholomew, lowly though he is. The king is much less prominent here than in the picture of him looking down on his subjects.

Bartholomew's humility, especially as opposed to the king's snobbery, marks him as a particularly worthy hero of a fairy tale, as does his action of starting out early, "just after sunrise," on a Saturday morning to sell a basket of cranberries at the market. On a day generally associated with leisure, Bartholomew is prompt and happy to be going to work, doing the economic business of his family. He is also a good son, since "he was anxious to sell them quickly and bring the money back home to his parents." This is not the action of a boy out to seek his fortune, or of a malcontent or abused child who wants out of the family home at any cost. The fact that his pace quickens as he approaches the town only underscores his appropriateness as a virtuous, if otherwise unknown, hero. Though Seuss's language describing his attitude—"He felt very happy"—is unusually flat, yet Bartholomew's character is anything but.

But the language that signals the change in Bartholomew's otherwise unremarkable history is marked by heavy alliteration and clearly indicates a change in the formerly calm conduct of the story: "The sound of silver trumpets rang through the air. Hoof beats clattered on the cobbled streets." The change in the level of diction, from pedestrian to highly literary, marks the complication in the story. The king's arrival in the town is signaled not only by the trumpets but also by the cry to make way for him.

But this royal procession makes a remarkable stop, remarkable not only for processions, but also for Dr. Seuss, whose usual method of conducting a parade is to let it proceed forward with increasing speed. But this one is stopped dead in its tracks, and even backs up, compounding its unusualness, in order to look at Bartholomew with the hat still on his head, even though he is shown earlier reaching up to doff his hat, along with everyone else in the picture, to honor the king.

The king's question, "Do you or do you *not* take off your hat before your King?" indicates his haughty assumption that all his subjects belong to him. But Bartholomew's answer in just the same terms indicates his reverence and obedience, as does his address to the king. "Sire . . . I *do* take off my hat before my King." The king is his sovereign, no matter how rudely the king treats him. Bartholomew's virtue does not lie either in his cleverness in answering or in his defiance; the magic of the story is not of his making, as is the case with Marco in *Mulberry Street.* No matter what happens, Bartholomew is never rude or ruffled; like Dorothy in *The Wizard of Oz,* he is the self-assured American child, at home and at ease everywhere, even when not at home.

To be sure, the king is justly confounded by the presence of the two hats, as is Bartholomew. But his quickness to anger contrasts with Bartholomew's persistent calmness, as is clear in his subsequent action of ordering Bartholomew's arrest. In this action the king indicates his propensity to anger and hasty judgment before gathering all the facts of the situation. That he calls Bartholomew an "impudent trickster" indicates his inclination to premature character assassination. The captain of the King's Own Guards is simply following the example of his king when he carries Bartholomew away by catching him by the shirt and whisking him away so hard that he loses his basket. The cranberries not only scatter, they suffer the indignity of rolling "down into the gutter," thus underscoring the king's disregard for his subjects and what they consider valuable.

Bartholomew is clearly in trouble, as indicated by the "black carpet" he is to follow to the Throne Room, apparently reserved for villains the way that the red carpet is reserved for dignitaries. Yet he remains self-assured by his own conviction of his innocence: "the King can do nothing dreadful to punish me, because I really haven't done anything wrong. It would be cowardly to feel afraid." This is no unreflecting simpleton who does not realize the gravity of his situation; he has assessed the dangers, and yet finds enough self-confidence to proceed. Though the king continues to use his most parental voice in addressing Bartholomew, his loyal subject refuses to be so cowed and continues to address him with utmost dignity. When the king demands: "Young man, I'll give you one more chance. Will you take off your hat for your King?" Bartholomew responds "as politely as he possibly could, 'I will—but I'm afraid it won't do any good.'" When Sir Alaric begins to tote up the number of hats, Bartholomew, "trying to be helpful," supplies the exact number of hats discarded at various points in the story. Bartholomew even apologizes that he escaped from execution because the executioner could not remove his hat. And he consistently tries to take off his hat, realizing the trouble he is in and trying to comply with the king's demands throughout, even when the king requires him to play William Tell as both Grand Duke Wilfred and the Yeoman of the Bowmen try to shoot the hat off his head, and even when the king twice sentences Bartholomew to death, first by execution, then by pushing off the turret. Bartholomew's quiet dignity in the face of all odds contrasts vividly with the king's quick rages and childish frustration.

Bartholomew's lionheartedness and basic goodness are also contrasted to the spoiled impatience of Grand Duke Wilfred, who resembles Bartholomew in boyish stature and in his fondness for wearing a hat. But the young duke wears a lace collar, like a priggish Little Lord Fauntleroy, showing forth his false superiority. And he demands to play with Bartholomew as though he were a toy, a target with which the duke can practice his archery. Bartholomew reassures himself that the duke's bow is no threat, noting out loud that the bow is only a child's toy, and that, in contrast to the duke, he himself is strong enough to use his father's bow, a real weapon. Such an observation only enrages the duke, who is further exasperated by his inability to shoot the hat off successfully, even though he exhausts his quiver. The grand duke responds with a childish tantrum: "'It's not fair!' He threw down his bow and stamped upon it," unable to control his rage. But the reader knows that the whole situation is unfair to Bartholomew, and that the hero is more provoked than the Duke, yet responds with steadfast equanimity.

It is the frustrated and spoiled Grand Duke who suggests the two executions, though the king's reaction to the suggestions signals to the reader that the threat of death is not to be taken too seriously:

> "If I were King," whispered the Grand Duke Wilfred, "I'd chop off his head."
> "A dreadful thought," said the King, biting his lip. "But I'm afraid I'll have to."

The king's tone in sentencing Bartholomew is hardly regal; he sounds more like a parent ordering a recalcitrant child to bed: "Young man . . . march down those steps to the dungeon and tell the executioner to chop off your head." The executioner "seemed a pleasant man" and responds to the request for a head chopping with "Oh, I'd hate to. . . . You seem like such a nice boy," further undermining the threat and making him a sympathetic character for recognizing Bartholomew's virtue. He further indicates his compassion by shaking Bartholomew's hand and sending him back to the king, thus foiling the grand duke's plan to get rid of the hat, Bartholomew and all. Thus, the reader is assured that death is not a real threat, at least not death by executioner, and that Bartholomew's story will turn out all right in the end.

The king is further misled by his nephew's next suggested method of execution and is talked into it against his first initial response:

> "Uncle Derwin," yawned the Grand Duke Wilfred, "I suppose I'll have to do away with him. Send him up to the highest turret and I, in person, will push him off."
>
> "Wilfred! I'm surprised at you," said the King. "But I guess it's a good idea."

This time there is not even the dignity of a sentence; the regal quality of the king and his power has degenerated into childish revenge. The king accompanies the duke and Bartholomew to the turret. While the duke seems to have offered a large favor in offering to do the dirty deed himself, he also seems to take boyish, vengeful, glee in the prospect. The offer is unacceptable, but the king seems unduly ruled by his nephew and adopts the idea readily, after his initial expression of shock.

But it is the duke's childish impatience that is his undoing; he will not wait to push Bartholomew and the five hundredth hat off the turret when the king commands him to: "I *won't* wait. . . . That new big hat makes me madder than ever." That the king saves Bartholomew and punishes the duke by grabbing the duke by the lace collar and spanking him on his royal rear end is a satisfying end to the duke's brattiness, for the lace collar and the prominently displayed rear end have been distinguishing marks of the duke's person. The lesson that the king delivers to the "royal silk pants" is "that Grand Dukes *never* talk back to their King," a lesson that Bartholomew has already demonstrated he knows quite well.

The distance between the king's attitude toward Bartholomew—barely tolerating him and responding too emotionally, without listening to his loyal subject—and Bartholomew's attitude toward the king—tolerant, acquiescent, obedient—is emphasized throughout by the distance between the two in the pictures, at least until the end, when Bartholomew and the king walk arm-in-arm, Bartholomew bareheaded, the king wearing Bartholomew's towering five hundredth hat. When Bartholomew approaches the throne on the black carpet, the king, with his arched eyebrows, frown, and unpleasantly crooked nose, is clearly visible, staring across the page at Bartholomew, whose expression is almost invisible, given his distance from the king, and he, himself, is only identifiable by his red hat, with its tall feather. Only in one picture are the king and Bartholomew shown as friends, and that picture is succeeded by the one of Bartholomew returning home, hatless and wealthy, but happy to be back where he belongs.

The story is a good one for reading aloud, as May has pointed out,[5] primarily because it is a story, unlike *Mulberry Street,* which operates as an ever-expanding list. The cohesiveness of *500 Hats* results from its origin as a literary fairy tale; whereas *Mulberry Street* is more of a cumulative nursery rhyme. The only other children's books that Seuss composed in prose are the second Bartholomew story, *Bartholomew and the Oobleck,* and another literary fairy tale, *The King's Stilts,* which shares many of the qualities of the Bartholomew stories. But all of these books work well as read-aloud stories, unlike the Beginner Books of the later period, which are more designed for independent, silent reading by an individual child reader. Though Seuss is an able craftsman of the literary fairy tale, his fame lies in other areas.

Bartholomew is the first of Seuss's small but powerful heroes whose heroic qualities come from living the virtuous, though unexceptional and obscure, life. There is nothing that Bartholomew does to merit being chosen as the hero of a fairy tale; both before and after the story, he lives a common life of common virtue. But in time of crisis, his ability to muddle through without losing his temper or his bearings stands him in good stead, especially compared to the propensity of those larger and more powerful than he to lose control and common sense. Like the typical Horatio Alger protagonist, Bartholomew is the all-American boy, ready for all situations, who needs only for a situation to present itself for his worthiness to shine forth. A simple stroke of luck changes an unknown into a celebrity. As the underdog in his situation with the king, Bartholomew follows that archetypal pattern in American folklore of the small and modest individual who triumphs and even wins over his larger, more powerful, and pompous adversary by dint of simply carrying on as best he can.

The King's Stilts

Of all Dr. Seuss's books, *The King's Stilts* is the least known, perhaps deservedly so. It is another literary fairy tale in prose about a king with a problem and a helpful page boy. The story's resemblance to *500 Hats* is clear, but *Stilts* does little to distinguish itself as anything other than a spin-off from the earlier story. It is the first book that Dr. Seuss published with Random House, however, the publisher of all the rest of his books. It is the least of those books. On its own, perhaps it would have succeeded. But given its predecessor and the later, far superior, books that Seuss wrote and illustrated, plus the development of Bartholomew and King Derwin in *Bartholomew and the Oobleck,* Dr. Seuss shows his wisdom in not returning to the characters of *Stilts* for a sequel.

Even the names sound suspiciously derivative—King Derwin of Didd in *500 Hats,* King Birtram of Binn in *Stilts.* Birtram is a hard-working king who puts in a long day every day guarding his lowland kingdom by tending to the dikes and Dike trees, which keep the ocean back. The trees are particularly susceptible to attacks by Nizzards, buzzardlike birds who are kept at bay by the royal Patrol Cats, who are the king's personal charge. Each day, Birtram inspects trees, dikes, and cats. But at the end of his day, his page boy Eric brings him his stilts, and the king strides away with childlike intensity in his play. This situation would have continued indefinitely, except for Lord Droon, the king's gloomy prime minister, who is congenitally malevolent. He hides the stilts and fires Eric. Without his fun, the king declines in health and vigilance, to the point where the dikes begin to leak. But Eric saves the day, finds the stilts, returns them to the king, and rallies him to vigilance again. The cats follow their king into battle against the Nizzards, the trees and dikes are saved, and Lord Droon is confined permanently, sentenced to eat Nizzards three times a day.

The influences on the story from other works in English literature are obvious. First and foremost, the tale demonstrates the perils of "all work and no play." Like the boy with his finger in the dike in the Dutch folktale, Eric also saves his kingdom from flooding by a loyal action. The malevolent character, like Shakespeare's Iago or Malvolio, is evil simply because of a personality flaw, and is punished by a particularly apt sentence. Above all, the story demonstrates that a problem with the monarch leads to a problem for the whole kingdom, and that even a king should be diligent and hardworking.

What sets King Birtram apart from King Derwin is his childlike pleasure in the stilts. Derwin's problems result from royal pride and stupidity. Birtram is tricked, and the trick is particularly distasteful because of his innocent pleasure and joyful pursuit of a child's pastime, which he indulges in only after fulfilling his royal duties. He is a good king who governs well and wisely; he does not deserve what happens to him. Droon's action of hiding the stilts is as abhorrent as stealing candy from a baby.

But because the king is so good and so victimized, he does not hold the reader's interest the way that King Derwin does. Eric does not have to win over the king, as Bartholomew does. Eric's is a one-time rescue of king and kingdom. Birtram's willingness to participate actively and without reservation in child's play is engaging, but at the same time, limiting. It does not give the depth of character that King Derwin's faults do.

Again, the story is in prose, though some alliteration marks the tendency of prose to revert to poetry. Again, the pictures are pencil, with only red highlights to differentiate details from the shades of gray. Random House obviously thought the volume would be a commercial success. But Seuss's best work for Random House is hardly presaged here.

Horton Hatches the Egg

The inspiration for the first Horton book came fortuitously, in Dr. Seuss's studio, as one of his tracing-paper sketches of an elephant accidentally blew over a sketch of a tree. Answering the question of what the elephant was doing sitting in the tree yielded the story of the loyal elephant who would not abandon the egg of a bird for whom he had volunteered to baby-sit while the mother took a vacation.

Horton promises Mayzie, a bird labeled as "lazy"[6] in the first line of the book, that he will sit on her egg while she takes a break from her work. The vacation is prolonged by Mayzie's disinclination to work, and Horton endures storms, winter blizzards, the ridicule of the other animals in the jungle, capture by hunters, and exhibition as a circus sideshow because of his promise to guard the egg. When Mayzie returns, just as the egg is about to hatch, she demands it back and asserts her maternal rights. But when the egg hatches, the offspring is not a Mayzie bird, but an elephant bird, obviously having taken on certain physical traits from its surrogate parent. Mayzie is cast aside, and Horton is allowed to return to the jungle, progeny and all.

The story turns on Horton's promise and his repetition of it as a refrain in the story. His initial commitment to Mayzie is that "I'll sit on your egg and I'll try not to break it. / I'll stay and be faithful. I mean what I say." And Horton recalls this line throughout the book in its refrain: "I meant what I said / And I said what I meant. . . . / An elephant's faithful / One hundred per cent!" Horton also finds himself "seasick! / one hundred per cent!" a variation on the refrain. Yet his reward at the end is to be a proud parent, "Happy, / One hundred per cent!" for his faithfulness. Though the book teaches a lesson about faithfulness to promises and faithfulness of parents, the absurdity of the story is what carries it forward, and the refrain simply punctuates Horton's ridiculousness in a variety of situations brought on by his promise.

That the egg will eventually hatch is evident from the title of the book, but the reader loses sight of this promised eventuality in the face of Horton's tribulations, which are alternately uncomfortable, embarrassing, dangerous, and degrading for him. Mayzie's complaint that hatching the egg is work does not ring true, given Horton's inaction while sitting; that it is tedium is more understandable. But Mayzie's approach to Horton, in order to get him to take over sitting for her is inappropriate; even he protests: "I'm so immense!" and "*I* haven't feathers and *I* haven't wings." But Mayzie flatters him into taking on the job:

> I know you're not small
> But I'm *sure* you can do it. No trouble at all.
> Just sit on it softly. You're gentle and kind.
> Come, be a good fellow. I know you won't mind.

Though Horton does protest, Mayzie is right about him. He is gentle and kind and can sit softly enough so that the egg does not break. He does mind doing the job, but his faithfulness to his promise conquers his complaints. And though Horton says "I can't," clearly Mayzie knows he can. For all her broken promises that "I won't be gone long, sir. I give you my word. / I'll hurry right back," she is a good judge of character, especially with Horton. And while she decides never to return, and shows little maternal instinct, as the story progresses it also becomes clear that neither Horton nor the egg is the worse for her absence, bearing out her statement as she leaves, "Why, I'll never be missed. . . ." Mayzie may be faithless, but she can tell the truth on occasion.

Horton takes his job seriously, first by assessing the tree's strength and propping it up, and then by climbing up "carefully, / Tenderly, / Gently," at least as carefully as an elephant can, and sitting on the egg. The description of the ascent, "Up the trunk to the nest where the little egg slept," underscores the quietness of Horton's approach to it, and his quiet but admiring gaze on the egg in this picture shows that Horton is a lover of babies, even if they are yet unborn.

Horton assumes, once he is settled on the nest, "Now that's that. . . ." But at this point the story really begins. Not only is he in for a long sit, from spring through autumn and winter, complete with meteorological difficulties, but he is in for considerable social discomfort. Only at the beginning, in a thunderstorm, does Horton wish for Mayzie's return. Once winter comes, Horton begins his refrain: "I'll *stay* on this egg and I *won't* let it freeze. / I meant what I said. . . ." His resolve is particularly admirable, given that the egg and nest are not shown in this picture—they are covered with snow and ice, as is Horton, whose eyes and trunk are red with the cold, the only red details in the picture and therefore particularly noticeable.

By spring, Horton is physically more comfortable, but the animals in the jungle all come out to ridicule him, saying that he thinks he is a bird, as if he were suffering from dementia rather than loyalty. After they tease him, they all run away, leaving Horton to feel the social isolation even more bitterly. The illustration shows him with his back to them and a miserable look on his face, with the red egg and nest looking like a sore spot or a fiery burn on his tail. His social isolation is even more poignant, since the animals are shown turning their backs to him and running away as well.

But the turned back is an even more perilous position for Horton; the next page shows that behind him the hunters are approaching, at the same time that Horton is described as "So faithful, so kind." The juxtaposition of the cruelty of the hunters with Horton's innocent posterior makes the situation even more pathetic. When Horton finally hears the hunters, he turns and finds *"Three rifles were aiming / Right straight at his heart!"* that locus of his kindly feeling for the egg.

Horton's physical response to the hunters, as shown in the illustration, is particularly noteworthy here, since the hunters are not differentiated but are, rather, identical in their massed enmity toward Horton and the egg. When he turns ". . .with a start!" to see the guns pointing at him, Horton's four feet are all shaken loose with fright from the tree, and only his tail balances him on the tree. But as soon as he sees the guns, he turns to confront them with folded arms and a resolute look, to show his bravery. Though Horton might have seemed static in pose thus far, his changed positioning on the branch shows the artist's ability to exhibit the elephant's changing emotions, all the while perching him precariously on the egg.

Horton defies the hunters to "Shoot if you must." But the hunters realize that Horton's potential as big game is far more lucrative if they take him alive, and they resolve to catch him, not a difficult feat, since Horton promises them that "I *won't* run away!" Their motives are not simply his preservation, for they plan to "sell him back home to a circus, for money!" It is bad enough that Horton and the egg will be disturbed; that the disturbance is effected for pecuniary interests debases the elephant; that he will be made into a sideshow attraction because "he's terribly funny" debases his dignified faithfulness as well.

Horton travels long and far to the circus, as is made clear by the illustration of the hunters hauling him in a cart over a high peak, just one of "the mountains ten thousand feet high!" and then down the mountains to the sea, where he travels by ship over rough seas to New York. The summary line, in italics, *"And then the men sold him!"* makes the sale sound like slavery. That Horton is enslaved by the egg is a willing enslavement; the hunters' action simply complicates the matter and makes what was a private commitment to the egg a matter of public spectacle.

But Horton's travels are not over, for the circus owners take "him to Boston, to Kalamazoo, / Chicago, Weehawken and Washington, too; / To Dayton, Ohio, St. Paul, Minnesota; / To Wichita, Kansas; to Drake, North Dakota," in a tour de force of rhyming precision. Finally, the circus ends up in Palm Beach, which just happens to be the vacation spot that Mayzie has chosen. She spies the circus from the sky, where she is described as "dawdling along." From the picture of her looking down, it is clear that neither she nor the viewer can see Horton. She simply stumbles on him, rather than zooming in to reclaim her progeny. When she finally finds him, Horton is shocked, and he is not very assertive when she wishes to reclaim the egg. Though Horton exlaims, "My EGG! WHY, IT'S HATCHING!," Mayzie is quick to respond. "'It's MY

"No matter WHAT happens,
This egg must be tended!"

But poor Horton's troubles
Were far, far from ended.
For, while Horton sat there
So faithful, so kind,
*Three hunters came sneaking
Up softly behind!*

egg!' she sputtered. 'You stole it from me! / *Get off of my nest and get out of my tree!'*" Horton gives no verbal response, but only "backed down," both figuratively and literally, as can be seen in the picture. But when the egg hatches, the narration points out that the baby "HAD EARS / AND A TAIL / AND A TRUNK JUST LIKE HIS!" The elephant bird, though it still has Mayzie's wings and feet, flies directly for its true parent, Horton, while simultaneously flying away from Mayzie. Its perch on Horton's trunk seems the appropriate place for it, for it shows that it has been trained to perch on a safe place, a place that also allows Horton to bear it in front of him like the treasure it is. Mayzie is shown in the corner of the picture, chagrined and ostracized.

The people of the circus complete the story by calling the creature what it is and explaining its strange appearance:

IT'S AN ELEPHANT-BIRD!!
And it should be, it *should* be, it SHOULD be like that!
Because Horton was faithful! He sat and he sat!
He meant what he said
And he said what he meant. . . .

The use of the word *should* here indicates the sense of rightness that both the characters in the story and the reader have that Horton is being rewarded for his faithfulness. The increasing emphasis on the word, indicated first by italics and then by full capitalization, gives a sense of climax to the story, and so, on the next page, when Horton returns home to the jungle with his progeny, the reader is not surprised that he is described as "Happy, / One hundred per cent." The variation on his refrain makes for the happy ending that the title hints at.

Of all Dr. Seuss's books, *Horton Hatches the Egg* most relies on typographical variations, turns of pages, and differing line lengths for the effectiveness of the verse. Though the verse is primarily anapestic tetrameter couplets, sometimes the couplets are divided, with the first line of the couplet separated from the second by the turn of a page, thus imparting a cliff-hanger effect to the earlier page, an effect Dr. Seuss elsewhere tries to create with the illustration. The text on several pages ends with ellipses, again imparting the cliff-hanger effect that urges the reader on. The poetic line is usually four anapests long, but by dividing the line in half and making it shorter, the rhythm of the line is more obvious and the block of text on the page less dense, giving a faster pace to the story. The typographical variations, such as italics and large and small capitals, also mark the accent. The punctuation—frequent use of ellipses and exclamation points— adds to the excitement of the verse, the ellipses leading the reader on to read more, and the exclamation points indicating both intonation and ends of grammatical units. Though the use of enjambment sometimes runs the grammatical unit beyond the end of the line to the middle of the next line, mimicking the ordinary rhythm and patterns of prose, the grammatical unit most frequently ends with the line, thus making for a readable text.

The illustration of the elephant in the tree inspired the book. But the illustrations throughout are less inspiring. Horton is the same elephant who appears in Dr. Seuss's menagerie as early as illustrations for his college humor magazine, though there is more attention here to his eyes, which are Horton's primary vehicle of expression, given that he must remain fairly inactive on the nest in the tree. The animals in the jungle all have the same eyes and expressions, which in this case may be visual indication of their solidarity in their opinion of Horton. But the three hunters are not individualized, nor are the people who come to the circus. One wonders if the lack of variety is a flaw, or is a visual shorthand for showing mob mentality.

The real triumph of illustration is in the egg and in the Mayzie bird. Mayzie birds apparently lay eggs worthy of Easter baskets, for this egg is red with white dots, and its hatching is accompanied by red and black lines radiating from it, indicating the vigor with which it will enter the world. Mayzie sits on the egg in the nest not as if she is nesting, exposing her breast to the egg, but as if she is using it as a stool, a particularly unmotherly pose. Her red tail feathers resemble stiff ribbons, which seem to decorate the egg and make it look like a gift, which it will be to Horton. Though it is infrequently seen in the pictures, since Horton covers it with his own rear end, the egg's presence is implied by the redness of the nest, emanating from the egg's redness. Though red color frequently makes the egg look like a sore point on Horton's tail, which it certainly may have been, the color also indicates the growing life within and the warmth of the egg as it maintains contact with Horton.

Besides the red tones, the only other color is an intense aquagreen, which in recent editions does not quite match the color on the cover. Far from soothing, the combination of the red and green has some garish effects. When the green dominates the page, sometimes as the solid background, its intensity can overwhelm. But the clash of the two colors, especially with the contrast of the white page, is appropriate, since it illustrates a preposterous story of an elephant hatching an egg, a story that will end at a circus with a preposterous offspring.

Though the story has its limits, it is one of the most remembered of Dr. Seuss's works, primarily for the admirability of the hero. Horton is loyal to his outlandish promise. He becomes a hero through his inaction, his willingness to persevere in spite of the odds and the ridicule. Of all of Dr. Seuss's heroes, Horton is the most like those of Frank Capra, the film director and Seuss's commanding officer during World War II. Capra's heroes are otherwise unassuming, commonplace people who, through a series of unwished-for calamities, find themselves forced into heroism. In fact it is difficult to call what Horton does heroism, since he really does nothing; it is in Horton's inaction that his heroism resides. Horton, and Capra's protagonists, do the right thing by those they find themselves protecting, and in the end discover, much to their own surprise, that they are celebrated for their deeds and rewarded for their efforts. But nothing in their lives would have predicted that these nonheroes would become champions; fate simply forces greatness upon them, and they muddle through to greatness as best they can.

3

The Books after World War II

During World War II, Dr. Seuss practiced his craft as a film-maker. Though he started with informational films for the army, he soon branched out into documentaries that won him two Academy Awards. During this period, he did not write books for children; nor did he continue the cartooning that had earned him a living before the war. The serious nature of his military service submerged his ability to write humorous books for children; the reading public also had other preoccupations that precluded much interest in children's books. But the military service provided a period of incubation for new ideas, both humorous and serious, which would appear in the children's books after the war. Some serious messages emerge in these books. The political implications of *Horton Hears a Who!* may escape the child reader, but are clear to the adult. The indictment of the materialism of American culture and its promotion of Christmas trappings in *How the Grinch Stole Christmas!* is damning. Overall, these books show a more complex approach to children and their literature, and more originality. The connections between Seuss's literary studies and these books are much less clear, while at the same time a Seussian sense of humor in systematic illogic emerges.

McElligot's Pool

McElligot's Pool is the first of Dr. Seuss's books to be recognized as meritorious by the community of experts in children's books. In this period Dr. Seuss became known primarily for his artwork, though the feat of using limited vocabulary to tell an interesting story in *The Cat in the Hat* directed some focus to his writing. But because his illustration style is so distinctive, so much so that one look for a reader identifies a book as a Dr. Seuss creation, the author is justly renowned for the illustration.

The winner of the Caldecott Medal for 1948 was *White Snow, Bright Snow* by Alvin Tresselt, illustrated by Roger Duvoisin. Though both author and illustrator are still known for their work, the book is not a great classic and certainly not a best-seller today. It remains a kind of historical relic, while *McElligot's Pool* still sells. Obviously, Dr. Seuss's continuing reputation, sustained through his other books, helps keep *McElligot's Pool* alive, but the book is justly esteemed for its own merits.

The story features Marco, of the earlier *Mulberry Street* book, here explaining to a local farmer why he fishes in a body of water otherwise known only as a repository of junk. While Marco is never shown actually catching a fish, he explains that he has every right to hope for a bite, given that he imagines the possibility of an underground stream beneath McElligot's Pool that connects to the sea, where a large number of strange fish are making their way directly to him. The underground-stream theory seems unlikely, yet Marco consistently points out that improbability does not mean impossibility. The strength of his fantasy about the fish, imagined in great variety and detail, sustains him in what seems to the more prosaic farmer a hopeless cause. But at the end, the farmer, if not convinced, is at least considering Marco's explanation of his perseverance, though the boy is shown in the same position as at the beginning of the book, with his fishing pole in the water waiting for a bite.

The story is clearly a proverbial fish story, and Marco does not even have the advantage of explaining about the "one that got away." But he has clearly in mind the ones that are coming his way, and Dr. Seuss's use of color in this particular volume is remarkable—and out of keeping with his earlier book illustrations. These illustrations use a full palette of colors and combine the harder, more definite lines of pencil drawing with the luminous, more delicate qualities of watercolors. Indeed, the use of watercolors here seems particularly appropriate, since water—the pool, the underground stream, the sea—is the dominant setting for the book. The translucent quality of watercolors mimics the natural effect of water on the objects in it, and the delicacy of the coloring marks this book as clearly different in the Seuss body of work.

The book also depends on the contrast between alternating two-page spreads using only black and white, and the others in full color. The alternation may have been dictated by the book's construction, higher costs having been avoided by not using full-color throughout. But the effect of the alternation is to bring extra attention to bear on *all* the pictures, since the contrast slows the viewer down, forcing the eyes to adjust and, therefore, to focus more clearly. There is no temptation to scan quickly through the pages, as might be the case with the routineness of either full-color art on each page or black-and-white throughout. The viewer here is nearly forced to stop and look at each page.

The dominant colors are green and blue, which are consistent with the aquatic character of the book. But the colors' richness and vibrancy are even more accented by the highlights of bright orange and yellow, the occasional delicacy of a coral-pink, and the definition provided by a black line. Though the sharpness of outline characteristic of a three- or four-color book, such as *the Cat in the Hat,* is missing in the colored pictures, the brightness of the page, which consistently lets the whiteness of the paper show through the watercolors, is startling and pleasing to the eye. Though the occasional land scenes are not as satisfactory as the ocean ones, relying heavily on the "Golden Book" style of art established by such illustrators as Leonard Weisgard, they are more than compensated for by the lushness of the sea life as Marco imagines it and as Dr. Seuss illustrates it.

Like the later *One Fish, Two Fish* for the Beginner Book Series, *McElligot's Pool* is a catalogue of fish, starting with the ordinary, but then progressing to the more fantastic. Like Marco's earlier tall tale in *Mulberry Street,* once this story begins, the fish progress from the small to the larger and more glamorous and gorgeous. Unlike the Beginner Book, the fish imagined here are more outrageous, but then, the limited vocabulary of a Beginner Book restricts description to such simple adjectives as "red, blue, old, new." The author was not so confined by vocabulary constraints in *McElligot's Pool,* so that "A THING-A-MA-JIGGER" which *"makes a whale look like a tiny sardine!"*[1] can be drawn and described as well.

As in many Seuss fantasies, each item in Marco's fish story is inspired by some small bit of reality, fleshed out by extreme, though logical or linguistic possibilities: a catfish, looking more feline than an actual catfish, inspires a dog fish to chase him. A jelly fish becomes pink because it is full of strawberry jelly. A sea horse suggests the possibility of a partner, "a fish / Who is partly a cow!" Sometimes the inspiration is geographic—fish from the Arctic look like Eskimo, fish from the tropics are "sunburned and hot." And sometimes Marco simply tries to outdo his last inspiration—a fish who travels by executing a human swim stroke is supplanted by a quicker fish who travels on skis, or a fish even stranger and more exotic because he comes from the place Marco imagines is the farthest away, Tibet. The penultimate stroke of imagination has to do with the size of whales—" / 'Cause there's *nothing* that's bigger / Than whales, so they say." But Marco is unwilling to stop with commonly held opinions, so he imagines the "THING-A-MA-JIGGER," to outdo the whales by size.

Though Marco ends his fish story with the Thing-a-ma-jigger, along the way he invents circus fish, who in punning fashion, come "from an acrobat school" and perform a balancing act. As he resorted to the circus for inspiration in *Mulberry Street,* so Marco returns to it in *McElligot's Pool*. Ort has observed that Dr. Seuss's art and primary direction in story telling resembles a "reviewing-stand and dress-parade" experience.[2] She has isolated the primary connection between Marco's different breeds of fish. Each marches in parade as a contrast to the one that came before. Marco wants to dazzle the viewer with the most amazing sights that he can invent, so the overall movement is to the largest, most extravagant aquatic life he can come up with.

And as in *Mulberry Street,* Marco's reason for stretching his stories so far is the incredulity of an adult. In *McElligot's Pool,* Marco is much more glib, less reflective about the quality of the story than in the earlier book, but still, he must justify himself to an adult, find some reason to explain what he is doing. That the story is so narcissistic, with all these wild fish making their way directly to Marco's otherwise unremarkable pool is consistent with the way that children imagine the world—it revolves solely around them, particularly for their benefit. Like Marco's story in *Mulberry Street,* where the parade goes by especially for him, the fish here exist solely for his benefit, as does the pool.

But the assuredness with which Marco narrates his story is what makes it convincing, and his anticipation of the adult farmer's doubts is a useful ploy in derailing those doubts. He admits to the farmer at the beginning: "It *may* be you're right . . . / There *might* be no fish . . ."; but he argues that any possibility, however improbable, is worth pursuing, *"Cause you never can tell / What goes on down below!"* Every possibility is turned into a positive probability by the use of the modal verbs *might* and *may*: "I *might* and I *may* and that's really no joke!" His choice of fishing holes has tipped the percentages in his favor: "One doesn't catch *this* kind of fish as a rule, / But the chances are fine in McElligot's Pool!" He posits all these possibilities as a reward for his perseverance at the pool: "If I wait long enough; if I'm patient and cool, / Who knows *what* I'll catch in McElligot's Pool!" Since patience, at least for fishermen, is widely viewed as a virtue, the least he can expect is some kind of bite, even though the similarity of the book's opening and closing pictures, with Marco still waiting beside the pool, might undermine another boy's confidence.

The farmer, who announces on the first page that Marco is "a sort of a fool!" himself looks quite foolish, and by the end, he is given no words to reply to Marco's closing contention:

> And that's why I think
> That I'm not such a fool
> When I sit here and fish
> In McElligot's Pool!

As if seated at a wishing well, Marco, and the reader as well, is sure that his wishing for these fish will make them appear. What the farmer ignores is that imagining all these fish, all bound and determined to be caught by Marco in McElligot's Pool, is part of the gratification of fishing. Just sitting and contemplating is as important as actually catching something. The farmer has some inkling that part of what Marco is doing at the pool is just simply making time to daydream:

> If you sat fifty years
> With your worms and your wishes,
> You'd grow a long beard
> Long before you'd catch fishes!

The tone with which he addresses Marco in this speech, using a parental, disciplinary "Young man" to open this statement, indicates the somewhat punitive tone with which he confronts Marco, as if to tell him that he is goofing off. Calling Marco a fool on the first page is hardly evidence of his courtesy, either. But Marco's story is another way of goofing off, of showing the fun involved in physical leisure while the mind is still active. In the end, even the farmer shows some evidence of having been converted to Marco's way of thinking.

The book is dedicated to Seuss's father, "T. R. Geisel of Springfield, Mass., The World's Greatest Authority on Blackfish, Fiddler Crabs and Deegel Trout." And Seuss admits that the story was inspired by a childhood fishing trip with his father.[3] Blackfish and fiddler crabs are actual species of sea life, though they are lesser known in parts of the world outside of Springfield. But Deegel Trout are purchased from Deegel's Fish Market, just as the author and his father did when this particular fishing trip was unsuccessful. The story has the flavor of the other books that bear some relationship to Springfield and Seuss's own childhood: most notably *Mulberry Street,* in which Marco's fantasy creation parades down a Springfield thoroughfare; *If I Ran the Circus,* also dedicated to Seuss's father, where again a young boy directs the most unlikely extremes of action in his fantasy; and *If I Ran the Zoo,* whose title reflects one of the elder Geisel's responsibilities in his job as director of parks and recreation in Springfield. Each of these stories features a young boy telling how he would make the actions of adults better, more exotic, and more glamorous if the world were his to operate, and each sounds suspiciously like a childhood reminiscence of Seuss's, brought to larger-than-life proportions by his adult imagination and illustration.

Thidwick the Big-Hearted Moose

One of Dr. Seuss's least-known characters is Thidwick, though the author has admitted that the moose character is one of his personal favorites. Thidwick evolved as a lucky accident; while the author was on the phone one day with his friend Frank Warwick, Seuss doodled a moose with some friends in his antlers. Seuss started out calling the moose Warwick, but changed the name as the story evolved. That the story should have come close on the heels of the Horton stories is not surprising, since in temperament the two are quite similar, as are their adventures; even the primary colors for their stories, red and a deep aqua, are the same.

Thidwick is a moose with a large heart, at least figuratively. He lets animals roost in his antlers. The first self-invited guest is a Bingle Bug, whom Thidwick is happy to oblige with a ride. But the bug, without consulting Thidwick, presumes on Thidwick's hospitality and invites a spider, who weaves a web in the antler and invites a bird, who plucks Thidwick's head for materials for a nest, and then marries and invites his wife and her uncle. All of these characters welcome four woodpeckers, a family of squirrels, a bobcat, a turtle, a fox, some mice, some fleas, a bear, and a swarm of bees. Though Thidwick is ostracized by the moose herd for not getting rid of the uninvited guests, and is outvoted by the guests when it comes time for him to cross the river to find more food, his constant refrain is, "For a host, above all, must be nice to his guests." When the host is finally within gunshot range of some hunters, he tries to escape with his heavy burden of freeloaders. But he is not fast enough, and the only thing that saves him is coincidence: that very day is the time for the moose's annual shedding of antlers. Thidwick leaves his headgear behind for the hunters and rejoins the herd; of course, the guests, along with the rack of antlers, become the hunters' prize, and are shown on the final page hanging on a wall in the Harvard Club, "All stuffed, as they *should* be."[4]

Like Horton, Thidwick is a victim of his scruples; once started on a course of action, only luck gets him out of his overly zealous adherence to his honor. The other moose have the right idea when they tell Thidwick, "GET RID OF THOSE PESTS!" but Thidwick can only see that *"They're guests!"* Like Horton, Thidwick is victimized by a sort of bird—the one with the new wife and her uncle is a Zinn-a-zu Bird, with coloring, wings, and tailfeathers like Mayzie's. Like Horton, Thidwick is besieged by hunters, who are not so much interested in the animal as in its oddities. And like Horton, Thidwick is finally rescued, and the odious presumers on his good nature are duly punished.

But Horton is clearly the better known of the two, probably because his refrains are more appealing and more noble than Thidwick's, and because his story makes more sense to children than Thidwick's. The dignity of faithfulness to promises and of small people's rights appeals to a child's sense of fairness and consistency in the world, and are themes which are frequently acted out in the course of everyday living. On the other hand, to a child, being hospitable to guests may simply mean sharing toys. It certainly does not mean subjecting oneself to peril, especially since the peril could easily be avoided by a shake of the head.

Thidwick's story is also simpler and, therefore, less interesting than Horton's, having one main episode, as opposed to two or three parts to Horton's in *Egg*. The moose's reward at the end is simply to be left to graze on moose-moss with his herd. There is no great tribute to celebrate his virtue. The joke about the Harvard Club and the old boys who come hunting for Thidwick will make little sense to children. In the end, the change of name from Warwick to Thidwick seems appropriate, for the latter name suggests how it came to pass that Thidwick gets in trouble—by his thick wit. At no point does he stand up for his beliefs; he simply succumbs to them in a most unheroic fashion.

Bartholomew and the Oobleck

Dr. Seuss returned to Bartholomew and the kingdom of Didd once again after World War II. *Bartholomew and the Oobleck* makes some slight changes in the characters from the earlier *Five Hundred Hats of Bartholomew Cubbins* to tell the first of the Dr. Seuss ecology stories. Oobleck, much like the pink bathtub ring in *The Cat in the Hat Comes Back,* is an unknown, unidentified substance that comes out of the sky like rain, but is much more viscous and sticky, and definitely more green. Though the nature of Oobleck is not investigated in the book, only its consequences, the sticky, confounding nature of the substance is clear from the cover of the book, where someone is shown running, without being able to see, for the Oobleck covers his body from his head to his knees, with Bartholomew looking on in surprise. That the Oobleck is a menace is clear from the title page as well, where a large drop of it from an upper window threatens to engulf a small, frightened Bartholomew below.

Oobleck is made by King Derwin's magicians at his request. During "The-Year-the-King-Got-Angry-with-the-Sky,"[5] King Derwin, bored with the spring rain, the summer sun, the autumn fog, and the winter snow, orders his magicians to make something new come down from the sky, which he perceives to be his domain to tamper with as he chooses. They brew up Oobleck, which they frankly admit they have never made before. The king is pleased, for he thinks its uniqueness will make him the mightiest king who ever lived. But the sticky stuff proceeds to precipitate, first lightly drizzling, then coming down like a blizzard, until everything in the kingdom is stuck in place, including the king. Bartholomew forces the king to admit the error of his ways by saying "I'm sorry," and these simple words, like magic, melt the Oobleck away. The King then proclaims a new national holiday, in honor of "the four perfect things that come down from the sky," and is seemingly converted from his egomaniacal ways.

That Bartholomew will be the one to save the day is clear from the first page of the book, where the unidentified "they" of rumor and mythology have once again noted Bartholomew's accomplishments in the history of the kingdom of Didd: "And they still talk about the page boy, Bartholomew Cubbins. If it hadn't been for Bartholomew Cubbins, that King and that Sky would have wrecked that little Kingdom." Not only is Bartholomew already destined to be the hero, the Oobleck's potency is also made clear, since it comes from the sky and can destroy the kingdom.

Bartholomew has been promoted to page boy since his appearance in *Five Hundred Hats,* and has acquired some new clothes, with a shirt and vest that make him look something like a cleric with a collar and stole. His new hair style, brushed up and away from his face, makes him look older, as befits his considerable influence over the king. Though Bartholomew's primary role in *Oobleck* is to stand vigilant at night over the kingdom, waiting for the Oobleck to appear, he is also a royal Paul Revere, trying to alert the kingdom to the dangers of Oobleck, and a surrogate parent to the childish king. Like a good parent, he lets the king learn from the consequences of his actions but forces him to consider what he has done before it is too late, rather than letting him proceed further with a course of action that has already proven dangerous. And like the parent of an overly excited child, Bartholomew calms the king to sleep, though "it took Bartholomew a long time to get the excited King to sleep that night" after the magicians promise to make Oobleck.

The motivation for the king's anger at this particular moment in the kingdom's history is not clear, though his chronic tendency to fits of pique is. "Bartholomew had seen the King get angry many, many times before. But *that* year . . . Bartholomew Cubbins just didn't know what to make of it." It seems that the king is suffering from fits of doubt about his might, and fits of boyish boredom. In fact, when he has the idea to ask his magicians for help, and when they promise him Oobleck, the pictures on the corresponding pages show his face exhibiting particularly boyish glee. But that the boy will save the king from his boyishness is clear from the picture on the first page, where Bartholomew looks up thoughtfully at the king, while the king looks up angrily at the blankness of the page above him. Bartholomew is clearly in command of himself and the king, who even from the first page is verging on being out of control.

Though Bartholomew clearly speaks his mind to the king, unlike his actions as a more subservient subject in *Five Hundred Hats,* he is still appropriately reverent. He tells the king that it is impossible to have something new come down from the sky, but he does it by addressing the king as "Sire." When the Oobleck first appears, Bartholomew asks if it is "safe" rather than asserting his own estimation that it is otherwise, while the king proclaims it safe without any real knowledge of it. It is not until the king attempts to make the Oobleck go away, by trying to recall the nonsensical magic words of his magicians, that Bartholomew no longer controls himself: "Bartholomew Cubbins could hold his tongue no longer. 'And . . . [the Oobleck is] going to keep on falling . . . until your whole great marble palace tumbles down! So don't waste your time saying foolish *magic* words. YOU ought to be saying some plain *simple* words!'" The simple words that Bartholomew has in mind are words of apology, and to say that he is sorry is, as Bartholomew points out, the least that the king can do, given that the imminent destruction of the kingdom is the king's responsibility. The king objects to such discipline, not because Bartholomew is out of place, addressing his king so vehemently, but because "Kings *never* say 'I'm sorry!' and I am the mightiest king in all the world!" Bartholomew, of course, disputes the king's self-perception, pointing out that the king is covered with Oobleck and is unable to move. Bartholomew confronts him with his failure not only as a king but as a complete human being, for "if you won't even say you're sorry, *you're no sort of a king at all!*" Though Bartholomew turns his back on the king at this point, both symbolically and literally, the king is moved from his arrogant position, and breaks down in tears, green ones that resemble the Oobleck. The king summons Bartholomew back: "Come back, Bartholomew Cubbins! You're right! It *is* all my fault! and I *am* sorry! Oh, Bartholomew, I'm awfully, *awfully* sorry!"

The apology not only permits Bartholomew to return to his post as page boy, it also effects the removal of the Oobleck, as though apologies were the equivalent of a magic antidote. "Maybe there *was* something magic in those simple words, 'I'm sorry.'" But the effect is obvious: "They say that all the Oobleck . . . just simply, quietly melted away." Seuss waffles about the effectiveness of the magic in the apology by reporting its effect through the agency of the "they" of rumor. "But they say that as soon as the old King spoke them . . . the falling Oobleck blobs grew smaller and smaller and smaller." But still, the story would not have a resolution if what "they" say were not true, and so it seems that even though the narrator intrudes with a disclaimer about the magic power of the words—"Maybe there was, and maybe there wasn't"—the reader is persuaded that, in fact, "I'm sorry" does have powers beyond those of simple apology.

In any case, the king takes Bartholomew's advice, and even persists in following Bartholomew's lead like a docile child, for the story ends with the proclamation of a new national holiday in the kingdom of Didd: "And then, they say, Bartholomew took the old king by the sleeve . . . and led him up the steps of the high bell tower. He put the bell rope into His Majesty's royal hands and the King himself rang the holiday bell," in direct contrast to his earlier order that Bartholomew should convey the order to the royal bell ringer to ring the bell to proclaim the holiday in honor of the Oobleck.

The story as a whole acts as an explanation of why the kingdom of Didd has a national holiday in honor of such pedestrian, "old-fashioned things . . . the rain, the sunshine, the fog and the snow": It is because of Bartholomew's levelheaded approach to the Oobleck, and because of the near disaster caused by it and by the king's inordinate pride in it and in his own might. But in the end, the king has learned how to apologize, and has realized that the "four perfect things that come down from the sky" have no reflection on his own might, and "were good enough for any king in all the world, especially for him, old King Derwin of Didd."

The agency by which the king obtains the Oobleck is the magic magicians, who make a reappearance from *Five Hundred Hats*. In the earlier book, the magicians promise that they can get rid of Bartholomew's hat, but that their spell would take "just ten short years" to work. Here they are more effective with their spells, working the charm to make Oobleck overnight, but their spells and chants indicate their peculiarly Seussian brand of magic. They do not rely on more traditional magic language like "abracadabra," but have other words that make them sound like bumblers. "Shuffle, duffle, muzzle, muff. / Fista, wista, mista-cuff." The magic words make them sound like they have difficulty moving, for they "shuffle" and "muff," and sometimes resort to powers other than magic, like physical "fista-cuffs." Their magic spell to make Oobleck shifts levels of diction, from the conversational to the formal and almost archaic, as in, "It sure smells dreadful, does it not?"

The magicians do not know much about Oobleck, which they admit never having made before, but their chant sounds more like a curse than a wish: "Oh, bring down Oobleck on us all!" That they chant that they are "mystic men who eat boiled owls" makes their magic even more suspect, for it is not clear from their diet whether they are just very tough characters who can even digest boiled owls, or whether they have ingested the wisdom of the owls along with the flesh. In any case, they are magicians and not wise men, for their knowledge is limited and they cannot advise the king about Oobleck, never having made or even seen it before, and they do not advise him about his overweening ego in desiring to be more mighty.

The Oobleck's first appearance is as "magic smoke, green, thick and hot!" which appears on the horizon of the illustration very

faintly, as just a wisp of green cloud. Bartholomew is relieved at
first, believing that the magicians have failed, and even the
reader might be convinced of this at first glance. Yet Bartholomew
notices—and the narration directs the reader to look for in the
picture—small, greenish drops. The Oobleck may start out as diminutive, but it gradually picks up size, speed, and noxiousness,
being described progressively as "greenish molasses," and then as
". . . gooey! It's gummy! It's like glue!" a rare instance of verse-
like alliteration coming through the prose narration. It is then
described as "greenish cupcakes," a "slippery potato dumpling
made of rubber," "greenish footballs," and "gooey asparagus soup."
These descriptions are both tactile and visual, and in a few cases
even disgustingly gustatory, the food references made more unpleasant by the green color. As descriptions, they are particularly
effective because they appeal to so many senses; that the last description includes "asparagus" is particularly suited to a young
audience, since asparagus is a vegetable, and an unpleasant
green one at that.

The Oobleck's particular shade of green is artificial, a bright
kelly green, one unseen in nature. That Bartholomew at first
doubts the possibility of finding anything new to come down from
the sky indicates that it is something out of the natural order of
meteorology. That the magicians do not know much about it and
that they cook it up until it smells "dreadful" make the reader
suspicious about it. Bartholomew's query to the king about the
safety of Oobleck calls into question its toxicity. The Oobleck's
precipitation on the kingdom while it is asleep makes the harm
it does even more heinous, for the kingdom is unsuspecting as
well as wrongly victimized. Everyone is caught in the Oobleck,
making its endemic nature the more potentially tragic, for it not
only sticks to the Captain of the Guards but also to those who are
less closely allied to the king, in fact to all his subjects, human
and otherwise: a poor robin at first, and then "there were farmers
in the fields, getting stuck to hoes and plows. Goats were getting
stuck to ducks. Geese were getting stuck to cows." The agricul-
tural functioning of the kingdom is at stake, as well as the functioning of the court, since the courtiers ignore Bartholomew's

warning to get back into bed, and they go out into the Oobleck anyway. That the king in the throne room is also inundated, as are his magicians, who are buried in their cave, indicates that only human efforts will help now, and royal or magical prerogatives will be useless.

The lesson taught here about the power of apologies is a particularly American one, for apologies are thought in this country to alleviate much of the harm done by a mistake. In this book, the apology undoes harm. The message here seems peculiarly political. The king is a megalomaniac, like Yertle the Turtle, who wishes to dominate everything in his kingdom, even the sky. The king even calls it "my sky," as though he could exert sovereignty over it. But clearly he is not foresighted enough to govern it wisely, or to see the danger of tampering with the natural order. He longs not only for the variety that Oobleck brings but also for its novelty; it is as though he questions divine wisdom in having only four seasons, and wishes to order up a fifth.

Clearly, in most cases, a simple apology would not undo the damage of the Oobleck quite so readily; but this is a fairy tale, although a modernized one, so "I'm sorry" can rightfully have such a powerful effect here. It is not clear whether Dr. Seuss had a particular political leader or a particular disaster in mind when he wrote *Oobleck,* but the message is a particularly modern one when viewed as a possible political message: no ruler has the right to proclaim himself the mightiest in the world. No ruler has the right to tamper with nature and to damage it. No ruler is above taking responsibility for his actions and apologizing when he is wrong. No ruler has the right to endanger his followers for his own personal aggrandizement. Finally, no citizen can excuse himself from his responsibility to tell the leader of the wrongness of his actions, no matter how small his own personal power in the political unit. As well as being a fairy tale, *Oobleck* is a morality tale, and Seuss preaches here more obviously than in his other books. Perhaps the destruction he observed in Japan during and after World War II made him particularly sensitive to the moral implications of leadership. Certainly the other political books of this period—*Horton Hears a Who!* and *Yertle the Turtle*—make a political reading of this book seem plausible. But the exact identity of the real-life counterpart of King Derwin and of his kingdom of Didd are not clear.

The language in this book is prose, but less archaic than *Five Hundred Hats* and therefore less redolent of the diction of traditional fairy tales. Alliteration is particularly in evidence here, and Bartholomew and the narrator resort to it often. Like ancient Hebrew verse and some imitations of it in English, the language takes on an archaic flavor in spite of its otherwise modern cast.

Like the pictures in *Five Hundred Hats,* the drawings for *Oobleck* are simple pencil drawings, relying primarily on pencil shading and the white of the page for subtleties. But the lines are much surer here than in *Five Hundred Hats,* with none of the overly detailed backgrounds that sometimes crowded the visual effects in the earlier book. Given the natural qualities of pencil drawings—no hard blacks, but only shades of gray, and no whites whiter than the page—the imposition of the green Oobleck is particularly dramatic, since it is not a modulated color in the book, except at the beginning, when it first appears as a wisp of smoke from the magicians' kettle, and then appears on the horizon. The green is solid and definite; it gradually overtakes the pages and dominates them, just as the Oobleck overtakes the kingdom and threatens to engulf it. The particular red of the cover, another bright, man-made color, is not repeated in the book itself, though its brightness accurately promises an active story.

Though the book was awarded the first of Dr. Seuss's Caldecott honors by the American Library Association for "significant contribution to children's illustration," the new issues of the book no longer carry the gold seal indicating the award. It is difficult to know why this distinguishing mark on the book's jacket has been dropped, since it usually reassures buyers that the book has been judged for its quality. There may be technical reasons, such as the difficulty of reproducing the seal on a nonfabric cover. It may be that in Dr. Seuss's popular success with the Beginner Books, critics and readers have forgotten this early award for artistic achievement. It may also be that nothing except his name is needed to guarantee the sales of a Dr. Seuss book. But at least in its own time, the book was judged superior in its illustrations, and so we ought not ignore the significance of the artwork at the time of publication.

The illustrations are particularly subtle, especially with the gradual introduction and takeover of the green of the Oobleck. The individual illustrations are much better composed than in earlier Dr. Seuss books, with less distracting detail and more variety of expression for the individual characters. The use of the three-color separation technique—the three colors being the white of the page, the black of the print and the outlines of the pictures, and the single-color tone—is exploited to particular advantage here, in a way that obviously impressed the Caldecott Award committee.

Like other literary fairy tales, this one relies on older, traditional tales for inspiration. Here the king resembles Midas in his desire for extremes; and Bartholomew, like Paul Revere, the boy with his finger in the dike, and the truth-telling child in Andersen's "The Emperor's New Clothes," saves the day by a combination of traditional virtues. The royal fiddlers—there are three of them—seem to have been borrowed from the nursery rhyme "Old King Cole." The royal magicians are knowledgeable, if obtuse, like Merlin in the King Arthur legends. The Oobleck, though, is a particularly modernizing touch, making the tale more literary than folk, with a more obvious, particularized theme than most folk fairy tales—the preservation of the environment.

In some ways, the closeness of the relationship between the king and Bartholomew depends on a foreknowledge of *Five Hundred Hats,* and certainly the later story has much more richness if the reader is familiar with the earlier story. But *Oobleck* is still capable of standing on its own, and the political implications of it make it an interesting story for both adult and juvenile audiences.

If I Ran the Zoo and *If I Ran the Circus*

If I Ran the Zoo is the last of Dr. Seuss's Caldecott Honor Books and marks the end of his period as an important contributor to children's-book illustration by children's-book experts. Though the quality of his illustration did not decline, with the publication of *The Cat in the Hat,* Seuss's reputation came to rest particularly on his language and his ability to compose in the easy-reader style. *Zoo* is also the last of Dr. Seuss's reminiscences about his own childhood, and though *If I Ran the Circus* is also dedicated to his father, the later book is much less clearly related to the writer's childhood than is *Zoo.*

Once again, the hero and narrator of the story is a young boy, Gerald McGrew, who looks younger than Marco because he is smaller and more wide-eyed, but who confidently takes on the job of zookeeper, at least in his imagination, and changes the way the zoo is run. He establishes a new kind of zoo, filled with fantasy animals that outdo "The lions and tigers and that kind of stuff," because "You see things like these in just any old zoo."[6] Gerald wants "something *new!*" in the way of animals, and by imagining how he will capture them and how the zoo's visitors' will react favorably to them, he creates for himself a new role as world-renowned wildlife hunter and expert. He first imagines that he will let all the old animals out of their cages, and then that he will replace them with all sorts of new, improved fantasy animals that will delight and amaze the visitors. He invents machines to catch them and machines to feed them as well. On the penultimate page, the zoo is no longer the City Zoo, but now McGrew's Zoo, though the final picture, which is the same as the first picture, emphasizes that Gerald's feats have all been in his own mind.

The book plays on the well-known theme in Seuss's books that children can imagine events and situations that are much more interesting than reality, and that these imagined events are certainly possible, though the child's plans for making them real may be sometimes vague or unrealistic. The amazing zoo is a perfect metaphor for many of Seuss's creations, which are sometimes simply wild beasts made even wilder or improbable manipulations of real-life beasts. The zoo allows Gerald a forum to show off his powers of imagination, and to receive the world's adulation for his animal finds, just as the picture book is a forum for Seuss to show off *his* powers of imagination.

In this book, some of the animals are inspired by strange words in the English language that have captured Seuss's fancy. *Bustard* is simply an obsolete spelling of *buzzard,* but the bird as Seuss draws it is hardly a typical vulture; its diet, "custard with sauce made of mustard," is clearly chosen for its rhyming qualities. Its companion beast, a *Flustard* is another way of spelling the past tense of the verb *to fluster.* Though the two animals do not resemble each other, the Flustard being a four-legged mammal, its diet of "mustard with sauce made of custard," is the reverse of the Bustard's.

Other animals imagined from odd words are the Mulligatawny, who is imagined as a yellow beast of burden with a "chieftain," as Seuss describes him, on his back, one with a turban and long mustache, as Eastern potentates are frequently pictured. That the animal is yellow and Eastern is consistent with its name, taken from an Indian curry-flavored chicken soup, which is usually yellow. The Iota, which comes in two varieties, is an animal with small eyes and a wild tuft of hair otherwise obscuring his face. Iotas, which are usually so small as to be negligible, are found in two nowhere lands, as described by Dr. Seuss: the ordinary variety is found "In the Far Western part / Of south-east North Dakota," while the more exemplary variety is found "In the north-eastern west part / Of South Carolina." The directionality of North Dakota and South Carolina serves to confuse the reader even further, as if the far west of the southeast were not already confusing enough.

The Mazurka is envisioned as a bird with several varieties. Gerald McGrew captures the tufted variety. And in quick succession, Dr. Seuss shows a Gusset, a Gherkin, a Gasket, and a Gootch, only the last of which is a made-up word; their escort of "eight Persian princes" makes their otherwise odd appearance seem possible, though exotic. That Gerald McGrew does not know the names of the princes only keeps the picture from becoming more obscure, since the four animals are not distinctly labeled, and eight princes with names listed would just further confuse. The mix of nonsense syllables—especially ones that sound similar to real words, like *preep* (rhymes with *creep*) and *proo* (sounds like *prude*)—with real words shows the ability of both Gerald's and Dr. Seuss's imagination to play with words and invent tangible equivalents by the suggestibility of the real words. It also shows Dr. Seuss's interest in words, which he claims originated with his schoolboy studies of Latin, which imparted to him an admiration and love of language and an awareness of its possibilities.

Though these animals are fantastic, Gerald's imagination does not stop with imagining what the beasts look like. In a tour de force, he shows that it is also possible to imagine machines that will catch them. For example, he invents a Skeegle-mobile and a Bad-Animal-Catching-Machine, which look like Rube Goldberg contraptions, flimsy and byzantine in construction, but capable of doing what they were intended to do—catch Gerald's fantasy animals. Gerald even invents places for the animals to come from, such as Zomba-ma-Tant, which sounds peculiarly French, though the native helpers Gerald finds there "all wear their eyes at a slant"; and the "African island of Yerka," the home of the Mazurka. Clearly some of the names are invented for the convenience of the rhyme. But some exotic-sounding places are quite real, such as "the wilds of Nantasket" and "the Wilds of Nantucket," both of which are a convenient drive from Springfield, Massachusetts.

Occasionally, Gerald's fantasy fails, as when he uses the Skeegle-mobile to capture a family of What-do-you-know and as when he finds "a new sort-of-a-hen" whose topknot provides a roost for another of the same kind of hen, "And so forth and upward and onward, gee whizz!" This animal has no name, which suggests that the picture of the animal may have come first. Sometimes words are changed, most frequently by the adding of suffixes, to make them rhyme, as with the *Obsk* from the Mountains of *Tobsk* who eats "rhubarb and corn-on-the-*cobsk*." The made-up rhyme words go on with *mobsk,* and *jobsk,* and Thing-a-ma-*Bobsk.* This rhyming device is most effective when the rhyme scheme that results is a falling one, with the accent on the syllable preceding the suffix. For example, the Russian Pa*loo*ski is bound for the *Zoo*ski Mc*Grew*ski, a rhyme pattern that sets up a series of trochaic metrical feet ending each line. The effect is humorous in

English, a language that is predominantly iambic. But sometimes the made-up terms and altered words simply indicate an otherwise impossible rhyming situation, where the author creates peculiar words that sound like real ones but whose actual function is more to get him out of a bind with the rhyme than to create humor.

Gerald's entire purpose in creating this zoo is to capture the admiration of adults. Initially, he praises the present zoo as "pretty good," and he notices that "the fellow who runs it / Seems proud of it, too"; the turn to the next page shows Gerald in the same zookeeper's uniform with the same look of pride. Though he starts imagining the alternative zoo because he wants some animals that are "new" and "un-usual," his motivation quickly shifts. The first animal, a ten-footed lion, will make people "stare, and they'll say, . . . / This Zoo Keeper, New Keeper Gerald's quite keen." People's reactions will be quite extreme, he imagines. "They'll be so surprised they'll all swallow their gum," and they'll "talk" and "gawk." But the sight of the animals will always lead them back to thoughts of Gerald: "*Then* people will say, 'Now I like that boy heaps.'" And his imagined admiration from them then spurs him on to greater feats of imagination: "What *do* you suppose he will capture next week?" and "When *do* you suppose this young fellow will stop?" comments that urge Gerald on to more wonderful, dangerous exploits, until he catches "The world's biggest bird."

At this point, Gerald's fantasy has brought him to the brink of history and mythology:

The whole *world* will say, "Young McGrew's made his mark.
He's built a zoo better than Noah's whole Ark!
These wonderful, marvelous beasts that he chooses
Have made him the greatest of all the McGrewses!"

With universal adulation, Gerald will have outdone his whole clan's history, even outdone Noah's Ark, judged to contain the most varied and complete menagerie. The progression from unusual animals to their unusual diets, to unusual places, to un-

usual machines, ends in typical fashion for a Seuss book, with the
largest animal imaginable—then a page full of animals and people all gathered together to look at each other in a carnival-like
atmosphere. But the ending is deflationary, as with Marco's fantasies in *McElligot's Pool* and *Mulberry Street,* with the same
technique of repeating the first picture as the last picture. The
use of primary colors in the book is reminiscent of *Mulberry
Street,* and the message is equally ambivalent: imagination provides sights and adventures more interesting than anything one
might see in reality, and at its best, piles one layer of fantasy on
top of another; but eventually, one must face up to adults and the
limitations of reality. The world of fantasy is limited to the world
inside the covers of a book, and Seuss signals the opening and
closing of both the story and the flight of fantasy with a picture
of the adult's and the child's actual situation.

It is possible that *If I Ran the Zoo* was designated a Caldecott
Honor Book because it is a kind of encyclopedia of all Dr. Seuss's
best imaginary animals, and is a typical Seuss story about childhood imagination. While the book is for children, the use of actual
obscure English words gives the book a level of humor not intended for children. And though the animals are exotic, none
looks particularly fierce. The smiling creature on the cover, probably some kind of a long-necked bear with bright eyes and a blue
nose, looks out at the viewer with particularly animated eyes,
suggesting that though Gerald's feats are described as daring and
dangerous, they really are not. The cover further suggests that
the story will provide much entertainment and amusement without threat. Some of the jokes in the book are visual, for instance,
the odd contraptions minutely illustrated rather than so described in the text, and the odd antler configurations for some of
the deer. These antlers form a maze of confusion above the heads
of the deer and connect them all together. Occasional stereo ypes
of native peoples—potbellied, thick-lipped blacks from Africa,
squinty-eyed Orientals—may offend some modern readers, but in
general, the book delights readers of several ages at several
levels.

If I Ran the Circus uses many of the same devices evident in *If*

I Ran the Zoo. The story concerns another boy's grandiose plans to run a circus in a vacant lot behind a local corner store. Though Morris McGurk is the ringmaster and the prime mover behind the list of attractions that will be presented at the circus, the main actor and real hero of the story is Sneelock, the bald-headed, pipe-smoking proprietor of the store and owner of the vacant lot. Morris hosts the circus, but Sneelock does the work and takes the risks—he serves lemonade and sells balloons, is an acrobat, a drum major, a lion tamer, an alligator wrestler, and a general daredevil. The irony of the whole story is that Morris is never shown talking to Sneelock. Morris simply assumes that Sneelock will want to lend his lot for a circus ground, and will be willing to do odd jobs as well as perform. Sneelock's appearance—smoke complacently rising from his pipe, closed eyes as though in revery, shoulderless, shod in what appear to be bedroom slippers—undercuts Morris's estimation of him as a hero, a circus star, and a willing and able participant in the venture. The only time Sneelock is shown with his eyes open, as though cognizant of Morris's outlandish plans, is on the final page, where he looks at the reader with skepticism, while Morris stands with arms spread, proclaiming the imminent arrival of the circus and its wonders.

Though Morris McGurk shares a Hibernian heritage with Gerald McGrew, it is obvious that the two are not equal actors in their stories, simply by the detail given to Seuss's drawing of them. Morris is little more than a fleshed-out stick figure, with little variety to his facial appearance, and with little more to do than stand with his arms spread. He does not go on the adventures that Gerald does, but simply stands to the side of the pictures and lets Sneelock do the work and get the crowd's adulation. But then, it is the crowd's attention to Sneelock that Morris uses to convince himself that Sneelock will of course participate in the circus. It seems that Morris is interested in having the circus come to the vacant lot simply as an improvement on the lot's present circumstance—abandoned, filled with trash, and forgotten behind a rickety fence and a store with no customers and an owner who appears to like it that way.

Morris proceeds with his fantasy with the typical optimism of youth. He imagines that it will take him only "a half hour's work,"[7] though he at least admits that he must work, to cut down a tree, and "haul off those old cars. There are just two or three," as though the afterthought makes his assertion of ease convincing, since he has clearly counted the number of abandoned vehicles. His subsequent assertion that after he removes the litter "*then* the whole place would be ready, you see . . ." belies what the viewer does see. Though Morris may be able to haul away the junk, the fence will still need repairs, and all the circus paraphernalia and personnel will have to be engaged and assembled before the circus can begin. And there is one crucial detail that Morris has overlooked—he must gain the cooperation of Sneelock, who stands in the picture unconsulted and unconcerned about Morris's presence and plans.

Morris, of course, does not measure the probability that his schemes will succeed, or plan for contingencies. He simply assumes that everything will go his way and that he will have "the World's Greatest Show / On the face of the earth, or wherever you go!" a show literally out of this world. He decides to name his show "The Circus McGurkus," an unusual Latinate twist to his name, making it adjectival and placing it after the noun it modifies. It seems clear from this verbal invention that Dr. Seuss again chose the boy's name for its ability to rhyme, although with some Latin-like modification.

And as in *If I Ran the Zoo,* some of the sideshow attractions and circus performers are chosen as embodiments of odd words— Hoodwink, Truffle, Flummox, Bolster, Spotted Atrocious, Grizzly-Ghastly, and Colliding-Collusions, who ride in racing cars called Abrasion-Contusions. The most visually interesting is called the Jott, who juggles marks of punctuation, "twenty-two question marks, / Which is a lot. / Also forty-four commas / And, *also,* one dot!" The small creature, looking like a potbellied Who, and being Morris's equivalent of a one-creature flea circus, does keep all sixty-seven marks in the air at once, and it is a tribute to Seuss's understanding of his audience that there are exactly the number and kind of punctuation marks in the picture that are mentioned in the text.

These word pictures are interspersed between the acts performed by Sneelock, which become more and more daring as the book progresses, from Sneelock selling lemonade (though in tremendous proportions—500 gallons) to Sneelock being shot out of a whale's spout into a fishbowl, like a man fired from a cannon turning into a high diver, combining two tricks in one. Morris's tone in describing Sneelock's feats becomes more and more assuming. In his first real action in the circus proper, Sneelock must gather a pot of hot rocks to feed the Remarkable Foon. The fact that the pot is much larger than Sneelock, and that he manages to hoist it, steaming hot, over his head, barehanded, is not mentioned in the text. But the picture here contributes to the overwhelming sense of his deed, even though he is simply tending to an animal. Morris narrates: "Of course pebbles like this are quite hard to collect / But Sneelock will manage, somehow, I expect." At least in this instance, he is considering the difficulty of the task he has assigned to Sneelock.

By the end, Morris assumes much of Sneelock, and disavows any consideration of how Sneelock will perform these amazing acts. Though Morris expects that Sneelock will dive *"Four thousand, six hundred / And ninety-two feet!"* into the fishbowl, "With his hair still combed neat," he does not feel obliged to consider at all how Sneelock will do this: "He'll manage just fine. / Don't ask *how* he'll manage. / That's *his* job. Not mine." In the corresponding picture, Sneelock is shown doing an improbable but nonchalant dive into the bowl, and Morris is shown doing his job—standing there as ringmaster, pointing the crowd's attention away from himself to Sneelock. Suddenly in Morris's imagination, Sneelock is not doing Morris a favor; he is simply doing his job, no matter how unlikely a job it may be for him.

The reader can imagine the kind of gesturing and noisemaking Morris has been going through while imagining his circus. The opening picture, showing Morris with his arm still gesturing toward Sneelock, though he now stands in the doorway of his store rather than in the middle of the circus ring, underscores the implication that this fantasy has not been a silent, motionless adventure through Morris's imagination. It has been acted out with all the commotion and sound effects a small boy is capable of, including an imitation of the ringmaster's voice and manner announcing the many deeds of Daredevil Sneelock, Kid Sneelock, Drum Major Sneelock, and so on. That Morris has been pictured gesturing broadly to the audience throughout his fantasy suggests that he has been acting out his fantasy, to Sneelock, though the boy has been unaware of the extent to which he has been caught up in his invention. Though in the final picture Morris has his eyes closed in the smug self-assurance that

> Why! He'll be a Hero!
> of *course* he won't mind
> When he finds that he has
> a big circus behind,

in contrast, Sneelock's eyes are open. The game is over, and Morris is about to find out that though he has assumed that "Mr. Sneelock is one of my friends," he cannot be so sure that "he might even help out doing small odds and ends."

The book's dedication to "My Dad Big Ted of Springfield The Finest Man I'll Ever Know" suggests that Morris's confidence in Sneelock is Seuss's tribute to the expansiveness of feeling toward his father. Like a small child, Morris believes that Sneelock can do anything; though children lose such a grandiose view of their parents with age, both the evocation of Springfield in the dedication and the fact that Seuss addresses his father as "Big Ted" suggest that the book is a childhood reminiscence of his own estimate of his father. Certainly the idea of playing circus is one familiar to children, but this atypical imaginative reconstruction of what a circus would be like is a tribute to the father, and to his son's view of him. That there may have been such a vacant lot and such a flight into imagination from the more mundane reality in Springfield is underscored by Sneelock's appearance in another book, *McElligot's Pool,* where he has the same store, but is passed by as rapidly as the underground stream linking the fishing hole to the ocean passes under him.

That the book is highly derivative, simply spinning out another version of *If I Ran the Zoo,* is obvious from the title. There is no better vehicle than the circus or the zoo to describe the kind of story that Dr. Seuss tells—linear in narration, cumulative, garish, noisy, and active, with episodic plotting and abrupt endings. But Seuss had played out all the variations on those themes in these two books. Both books celebrate the wonders of the imagination and the pleasures that both children and adults can find through imaginative escape. Both books provide wish fulfillment in the adulation that the world gives the boys who are doing the imagining. But there were other ways to celebrate these wonders of the human mind, and other audiences and challenges to address. It was time for Seuss to move on to a different sort of book—the beginner reader.

Horton Hears a Who!

Once again, Dr. Seuss returned to a prewar character in the period after World War II, and again, he used this character to make a political statement. This time, Horton the elephant represents more than faithfulness. In *Horton Hears a Who!* he represents postwar United States in the international community of nations. The Whos of Who-ville are Dr. Seuss's characterization of the Japanese after Hiroshima, a people whom he found optimistic, hardworking, and particularly eager to vote in their elections. *Horton Hears a Who!* is Dr. Seuss's statement about the Japanese people. Though anti-Japanese feeling in the United States ran high both during and after the war, Dr. Seuss clearly found the Japanese admirable and America's relations with them worthy of preservation, in spite of public pressure in the United States to the contrary.

The story begins with Horton, once again having nothing to do, as at the beginning of *Horton Hatches the Egg,* simply enjoying himself in the jungle. While bathing in a pool, he hears a small noise, which he finds is coming from a speck of dust. By careful listening, he finds out that it is the Mayor of Who-ville, who asks Horton to protect his town. The other animals in the jungle once again ridicule him for carrying around the clover blossom onto which he has placed the speck of dust, and they manage to get the clover away from Horton and drop it in a large field. Horton persists and finds the Whos, only to be tormented again by the other animals, who this time restrain Horton while threatening to boil the clover in oil. But Horton manages to get the Whos to call loudly enough that all the animals can finally hear them and finally believe Horton. But it is not until every Who, including one small shirker, starts making noise, that the sound is heard.

After his military service in the Signal Corps making films for the armed forces, Dr. Seuss went to Japan, where he made an Academy Award–winning documentary on the Japanese, whom he found much more admirable and likable than propaganda about them in the United States had led him to believe. They are represented in *Horton Hears* as a small people, so small that they cannot be seen, but they can be heard by those with particularly good hearing, such as that of an elephant. They have a parallel civilization to humans, with families, towns, governments, and churches. The diminutive stature of the Whos resembles the Japanese at the time, not only because Orientals are physically smaller than Caucasians and blacks, but also because as a world power, the Japanese were without influence or sympathy in the world community after World War II. But the elephant, the biggest animal in the jungle, and certainly the only one in this story with any physical power, protects them, both from public disbelief in their existence and from total annihilation.

The message here is twofold: each person deserves safety, no matter how small that person is; and each person has a civic duty to help insure that safety. Horton's refrain, "A person's a person, no matter how small,"[8] points to the first moral, and points a finger directly at the United States as a superpower who must therefore also be a protector of smaller governments' rights to exist. The action of the story that takes place in Who-ville points to the parallel responsibility of the small governments to help take care of themselves, the second moral.

Seuss himself admitted that the story is a political allegory.[9] Japan had been ravaged by two atomic bombs during the war, and by strict international supervision after it. Yet during his visit there in 1954, he found the Japanese people optimistic, industrious in their rebuilding efforts, and committed to free elections, the government urging every citizen to vote. Voter participation in Japan, represented in *Horton Hears* by every Who participating loudly enough in a communal din that the outside world can hear them, stands as an object lesson to the United States, where voter turnout has always been less than complete, though the right to vote is much cherished. Watching this communal sense of responsibility unfold in the book endears the Whos to the reader in the United States, for the language of the book appeals to American truisms about universal participation in the rights and privileges of democracy. "And you very small persons will *not* have to die / If you make yourselves heard! *So come on, now, and TRY!*" and "Are you sure every *Who* down in *Who*-ville is working? . . . Is there anyone shirking?" and "We've GOT to make noises in greater amounts! / So, open your mouth, lad! For every voice counts!" That the Whos' efforts to save themselves are rewarded makes the story particularly poignant. American readers, who consistently love the triumph of the small against the large, and who root for the underdog even against the most terrible odds, find particularly gratifying the narrator's pronouncement that "their whole world was saved by the Smallest of All!" Knowledge of the historical parallels is not necessary to see the point of the story, and some readers may be shocked to see the Japanese, propagandized during the war as evil, inscrutable devils, portrayed so favorably. Though the Japanese did not have to prove their existence, they did have to justify it before the world, given the atrocities committed by their government in World War II; Seuss, who saw through the wartime propaganda, successfully helps their cause here by using American commonplaces to describe former archenemies.

The Whos are also favorably portrayed in the kind of little world that they live in. When shown against the backdrop of the whole jungle, they are hardly visible, but when Seuss brings his microscopic vision to bear on their world, they are clearly imagined, with families, buildings, and leisure pursuits. However, even in the close-up illustrations of their world, they are still small, certainly smaller than the small animals, the monkeys and young kangaroo, shown in the jungle pictures. The use of the pastel tones of the colors shown in the jungle to illustrate Who-ville also makes their world seem smaller, less vivid, though no less fully illustrated.

As Horton gradually gets a clear picture of what Who-ville is like, the pictures of Who-ville become more fully detailed. Though at first all he imagines is a small, wispy creature on the face of an otherwise uninhabited, undeveloped planet, gradually Horton realizes that the Whos have families, which then appear in the illustrations. The mayor himself tells Horton that his actions have "saved all our houses, our ceilings and floors. / You've saved all our churches and grocery stores," thus helping Horton to fill in the details. The close-up of Who-ville not only shows the Who buildings, which are architecturally peculiar, since they do not have angles but are composed of arches, but also the Whos engaging in everyday activities, such as mowing the lawn, painting the buildings, taking care of children, and playing tennis and football, although with some oddly shaped athletic equipment. The face of the Who planet changes, though Horton's initial imaginative constructions of the planet are correct: there is "some poor little person who's shaking with fear," but there is more than one inhabitant of the little world. Horton then imagines that there is "A family with children just starting to grow"; in fact, there are many families. Their existence has been guaranteed by the gentle giant of an elephant, whose ability to imagine the planet full of pitiful creatures—not just small people but people filled with fear, not just families but families with children who are only just getting a chance at life—guarantees the readers', if not the jungle animals', sympathy.

Horton's feeling of obligation to the Whos is almost unreasoning; he feels the responsibility because the initial voice he hears comes from a "creature," a living thing that, because of the sheer fact of its existence, has rights. He feels the obligation too because the dust speck is powerless to navigate, and because "I'm bigger than they." Once the mayor has made clear contact with Horton, the obligation is one taken on willingly, not just as an unthinking obligation: "I *can't* put it down. And I *won't!*"

Horton, the kind and gentle giant, is the perfect hero for this story, because as the reader will recall from *Horton Hatches the Egg!* he is an "elephant faithful, one hundred per cent." Once the mayor can talk to Horton, he extracts a promise from him that the reader knows will be kept: "You're safe now. Don't worry. I won't let you down." The last part of the promise is meant both figuratively—that Horton will live up to his promise—and literally—that Horton will not put the speck of dust down, where it might come to harm.

But just as Horton makes his promise, the monkeys of the story, the Wickersham Brothers, begin taunting Horton and asserting that he is only making up the story: "This elephant's talking to *Whos* who are *not!*" The Whos' name suggests that they are persons and that they have voices that can call out—like "yoo-who." Because the Wickersham Brothers cannot perceive the physical evidence of the Whos, their voices, the monkeys deny them existence. They also resolve that neither Horton nor the Whos can be left in peace, in Horton's fantasy, if that is what they choose to believe that Horton is engaging in. They determine that "*we're* going to stop all this nonsense!" by giving the clover to an eagle who will drop it a large field, thereby both destroying Who-ville and frustrating Horton's commitment to maintain protection over the town.

The eagle is named Vlad Vlad-i-koff and is described as "black-bottomed," as one might suppose that a villain would be. It is possible that Seuss is pointing to some Russian intervention against Japan after World War II, but the exact parallel in history is not clear. Perhaps the evil eagle and his name are simply a stroke of fantasy. But the depth of the eagle's villainy indicates how far partners in international alliance may have to go in order to protect each other and destroy their enemies. Even though Who-ville is negligible in size and influence, still Horton suffers much to protect the town: "Horton chased after, with groans, over stones /

"You mean..." Horton gasped, "you have *buildings* there, *too?*"

"Oh, yes," piped the voice. "We most certainly do....
"I know," called the voice, "I'm too small to be seen
But I'm Mayor of a town that is friendly and clean.
Our buildings, to you, would seem terribly small
But to us, who aren't big, they are wonderfully tall.
My town is called *Who*-ville, for I am a *Who*
And we *Whos* are all thankful and grateful to you."

And Horton called back to the Mayor of the town,
"You're safe now. Don't worry. I won't let you down."

That tattered his toenails and battered his bones. . . ." The corresponding picture shows Horton and the eagle traveling on a page of solid blue, with only the whites of their eyes and the pink of the clover for color contrast, the overwhelming darkness of the blue showing the unpleasantness of this quest and its extreme duration, through a whole night.

Horton persists in his quest and finds the clover, though it takes him all day and though he must examine three million clovers to find it. Once again, he demonstrates the extent to which faithful friends must go in their promises. But while he is shown in the page before as tired, sweaty, and frustrated at noon, when he finally finds the Whos on the next page, at the end of the day, his appearance is once again animated and rejuvenated. The plea of the mayor at this point is simply guardianship. The Whos only want protection while they tend to rebuilding—no reparations, no assistance, simply vigilance: "Will you stick by us *Whos* while we're making repairs?" Horton answers them in the same terms in which he has been addressed by them: "Of course I will stick. / I'll stick by you small folks through thin and through thick!"

The animals of the jungle think that Horton's persistence has reached the level of insanity, and that his guardianship is disturbing their "peaceable jungle," a verbal reminiscence of the nineteenth-century pictures of the "peaceable kingdom" of God, where "the lion will lie down with the lamb." Here the reminiscence is ironic, for the other animals will not abide peaceably with Horton and the Whos; earlier in the book, they have rejected Horton's plea: "as a favor to me, / Try not to disturb them. Just please let them be."

Instead, the Wickersham Brothers, along with their relatives, who all look the same, join with the kangeroos to cage Horton and boil the clover in Beezle-Nut Oil. They seem to be overreacting to the same degree that they perceive that Horton is overreacting, and their plan to torture Horton by making him watch while they boil the Whos is particularly vindictive. But the threat, though temporarily serious, is really not so in the final analysis. Horton looks out at the reader from cover, assuring that he does hear the Who of the title, and assuring contact with and sympathy from the reader throughout. His perseverance is clear, and his over-powering bulk and continuing gentleness will guarantee that the Whos will be all right.

At this point begins the parable about voting. Each Who must stand up and make a noise, a communal chant that will make sure that the larger animals, even those without Horton's over-large ears, will be able to hear them. Each voice, each effort counts, and everyone must be heard in order for the entire community to be heard. The parallel between speaking up and voting is one that almost reaches the level of cliché, except that it is not just adults but also children who must participate here. Jo-Jo cannot be an innocent bystander, simply playing with his yo-yo; even children have an obligation. But when they exercise their powers, they can be heroes: "That one small, extra Yopp put it over!"; "And their whole world was saved by the Smallest of All!," a particularly poignant and heroic act, since the Whos are so small, and Jo-Jo even smaller. And by this one effort, Jo-Jo justifies the entire Who existence: "They've proved they ARE persons, no matter how small."

The political implication is clear, that all peoples and cultures have rights, simply because of their existence, even small, otherwise powerless people. But the moral is also one designed to interest children, to whom the theme of the large being overcome by the small has intuitive appeal. The theme has been around as long as the David and Goliath story, and it appeals to anyone who has felt powerless in the face of large obstacles of life. The theme is particularly attractive to Americans, who since their revolution have seen themselves as a small, scrappy band of patriots, who by perseverance and justness of cause beat the larger forces of the British Empire. Though there have been isolationist moments in American history, the appeal of smaller nations to be protected by the larger world powers has always brought popular support from United States citizens, and Horton is no exception to this patriotic appeal.

The ending brings a quick climax, then denouement, separated from each other only by a page turn, and consisting of less than ten lines. The Wickersham Brothers are all shown looking and listening excitedly to the voice emanating from the dusty speck on the clover. The kangaroo and her child, described elsewhere as being "sour," are shown with delighted, surprised expressions. The mother kangaroo resolves, "From now on, I'm going to protect them with you!" Her offspring correspondingly resolves, "ME, TOO! / From sun in the summer. From rain when it's fall-ish, / I'm going to protect them. No matter how small-ish!" The final picture shows Horton and the two kangaroos watching proudly over the speck, with the younger kangaroo holding an umbrella over it. With three such large characters dedicated to vigilance over such a minuscule item, the reader is assured that the Whos will receive protection, if not overprotection.

The assembly of kangaroos is an important one, whether the story is read as a political allegory or whether it is seen in more mythic, generalized proportions. Only on the final page are the two, mother and child, shown with different expressions. Before that point, the mother has taken the lead in commenting on Horton and his actions, and the sameness of expression on their faces serves to emphasize the lack of thought on the part of the child; his only lines have been, "Me, too" and "Me, neither." Like a less powerful satellite nation, the young kangaroo has depended on the adult not only for the necessities of life, as suggested by the mother carrying the child in her pouch, but also for his opinions. It is not until the last page that the child has any extensive speech of its own, and then, though he has taken the lead from the parent, the addition of the umbrella to protect the Whos is the child's own idea.

Even without consideration of the possible political meanings of the young kangaroo, the offspring still has meaning in the story; though Horton keeps asserting that "a person's a person no matter how small," the young kangaroo seems not to understand the implications of the refrain for himself. He is content to remain in his mother's pouch, with no thought as to what the destruction of little folks for no reason could mean for him. But finally, when even the Whos can make themselves heard, the young kangaroo finds his language, too, and shows his personhood by taking an active role in guarding those even smaller than he.

The colors of the book, bright blue and red, sometimes toned down to pastel tints of the same colors, evoke a patriotic image. The line drawings in pen, without any of the preliminary, sketchy feeling of pencil drawings, make the lines hard and clear, with little shading, except for crosshatching, giving the book the same two-dimensional aspect found in the Beginner Books. Though the deep cast of the blue makes the book seem elegant, the vibrancy of the red, especially when used as the color for the jungle flowers and trees, makes the setting exotic. And Horton, without any suggestion of the gray of real elephants, is a big white animal, dominating the page with his enormous expanse in several two-page spreads, his presence pure and unsullied by realism. The expanse of his ears, here looking more like angel wings, is played to full advantage, as are his eyes, which interpret for even the youngest reader his various feelings during the story. The large-page format makes the elephant seem even bigger, as he dominates many of the pages, at the same time it makes the speck of dust on the clover seem even smaller by comparison. If the reader were not initially directed by the text to look for the speck, its otherwise unprominent detail would be lost. The size of the page works to the Whos' advantage when Seuss shows a close-up of their world, for such a large page can be filled with much detail from their lives and with many of them. The lines in such drawings are much finer than those in the jungle, which tend to be bold, with less detailing.

In fact, the fine print in which the mayor of Who-ville "speaks" also guides the reader to scrutinize the Whos' world. The much smaller typeface for his speeches slows the reader down and makes him read more carefully, training him to look at the picture with the same kind of mind-set for close detail, and even to scrutinize some of the larger pictures as well. This change in typeset works particularly effectively with Jo-Jo's climactic "YOPP!" which is set in small caps, contrasting with the full-sized upper and lower case letters that describe the word's appearance in the jungle world. Though the letters are small, they are larger than the fine print of the Mayor's exhortation to him, and make clear that the sound, though large in Who terms, is still small, though convincing to the jungle animals. Jo-Jo's choice of exclamatory syllables is unusual, but the word has been foreshadowed in the text, first by Horton's hearing a faint "yelp" from the speck, then by Horton's being told by the eagle to "Quit your yapping," then by the mayor's observing that "*Every*one seemed to be yapping or yipping!" in Who-ville, and finally, by the mayor's discovering that Jo-Jo has a yo-yo, and is playing with it without a single sound, even "a yipp!" The "YOPP!" is simply the final step in the logical progression through the vowels, and is a louder, lower-sounding word than either *yap, yelp,* or *yip,* the more logical sounding words for someone to make noise with. *Yopp* is a sound more likely to be heard than *yip* or *yap* because of the large vowel sound of *yopp*. At the same time, it is a nonsensical syllable, as befits this humorous yet meaningful story.

On beyond Zebra!

It is obvious from *On beyond Zebra!* that Dr. Seuss had been thinking about traditional education and its effects on children before he wrote *The Cat in the Hat.* Though the book is another catalog of strange Seuss beasts, its message about traditional school lessons and about the rewards of daring to go beyond the limits of common sense are clear.

Once again, a Marco-like boy appears and is instructed by an even younger boy, Conrad Cornelius o'Donald o'Dell, about his accomplishment in mastering the alphabet and what animal's name begins with what corresponding letter. When the Marco character claims that there is an alphabet that begins after the letter Z, Conrad is incredulous, but Marco proceeds and shows not only the elegant letters but also the preposterous animals whose names begin with the letters. Marco manages to assert his superiority over Conrad in the same smug fashion that Conrad has tried to assert his superiority over Marco at the beginning, but Conrad is won over in the end. He draws an even more preposterous letter than any Marco has imagined, impressing even the older boy and inviting the reader to figure out what the letter is and what animal it represents.

Zebra's attitude toward traditional book learning is embodied in Conrad, a little egghead, who must stand on a chair in order to reach the blackboard. In his tie and sweater, and with his neatly arranged hair parted in the middle, and ears protruding preposterously from the side of his head, he looks prematurely old, especially given the sparseness of the hair on his head. His overlong, overly formal name, which is never replaced with a nickname and never used without all four of the names together, only underscores his pretensions and foppishness. In contrast, Marco looks on respectfully, but stands relaxed, wearing a comfortable turtleneck and sticking his hands in his back pockets. As usual, Marco's hair is growing forward off his head without the intervention of a comb or brush. Marco is not even given a name in the book; he is simply the narrator, who speaks of himself in the first person. He has authority because he is the confident guide through the story. Conrad is trying to be older and wiser, as evidenced by the fact of his lecturing Marco about the alphabet, and by the certainty of his conclusions when he finally reaches Z and *zebra:* "So now I know everything *any*one knows / From beginning to end. From the start to the close. / Because Z is as far as the alphabet goes."[10]

But there are several details in the illustrations that undercut Conrad's self-assurance. First, in the opening picture, his terminal Z on the blackboard is larger and more askew than the other letters, with a tail that seems ready to zoom off the board. Thus, Marco is given a visual opening to begin his alphabet where Conrad's Z leaves off. In the second picture, Conrad draws a zebra, who looks knowingly out at the viewer, as if he knows more than Conrad, who does not follow the gaze away from himself but simply looks on admiringly at his illustration. And finally, Marco is not the only individual who is listening to Conrad's lecture. There is a dog, an undescribed, unspeaking companion throughout the book who accompanies Marco and Conrad on their journeys beyond Z and *zebra,* and who comments mutely on the action by his presence and facial expressions. In this second picture, the dog's expression clearly suggests his skepticism about what Conrad is saying.

Conrad begins his initiation to the alphabet beyond Z with a near pratfall: "Then he almost fell flat on his face on the floor" at the first letter that Marco draws on the board. Marco draws his letter with a flourish, incorporating two known letters, Y and Z, into a new letter. Other letters in his alphabet are less obviously derivative and are sometimes more elaborate, so the choice to start with the letter Yuzz makes Conrad's introduction to the new alphabet particularly accessible to him. Marco offers his explanation of the meaning of this letter and the habits of the animal who represents it. From this point to the end of the book, Conrad is mute before the marvels Marco shows him. Marco offers to introduce him to this other alphabet "'cause you're one of my friends," but the initiation is not only a gesture of friendship; it is also one of superiority. Marco clearly wants to show off his superior wisdom and his perseverance in going beyond the ordinary. His tone throughout is one of parental discipline: "It's high time you were shown / That you really *don't* know all there is to be known." At the last Marco says, "And I think, perhaps, maybe I did him some good . . . ," as though he is prescribing a dose to straighten Conrad out.

The two boys meet initially in an empty classroom, and Conrad assumes the role of the teacher, with Marco taking over after the letter Z. But there is no adult teacher in sight, though the blackboard and chalk clearly designate the space as a classroom. The reader suspects that Conrad is the kind of student any teacher would want in class, the kind any teacher would encourage to become a teacher himself—competent, well spoken, and confident. Marco's desirability as a student is more suspect: his learning takes place outside the classroom, and his attractive scampishness seems infectious, even to an entirely conventional star pupil like Conrad, who at the end outdoes Marco's antics by creating a letter even more splendid than any of Marco's. Part of Marco's attractiveness for Conrad, and for the child reader as well, is his convincing power of imagination, which breaks all the rules set by adults. That Marco is the leader is not surprising; like Tom Sawyer, he imagines glamorous, adventurous exploits for himself and his followers, especially as the exploits expand beyond the classroom and the traditions of the alphabet.

Marco's chief claim in favor of his alphabet is that it makes him unusual. As he explains to Conrad, "*You* can stop, if you want, with the Z / Because most people stop with the Z / *But not me!*" Marco asserts his individuality by disregarding commonly accepted wisdom. He thinks for himself and is rewarded for his iconoclasm. He likens the alphabet beyond Z to the explorations of the discoverers of the new world, and invokes one of their names like a rousing cheer or rallying cry: "So, on beyond Zebra! / Explore! Like Columbus!" And in fact, he does take Conrad, and the dog as well, to a new world "near the sun," a small planet with two creatures, "brothers called *VROOMS*." The planet is a small one, but arriving there means interplanetary travel, as is clear by the rocket ship Marco uses to transport Conrad and the dog. Of course, though Conrad and the dog are shown wide-eyed at the sights they see out the window, Marco is self-assured at the controls and does not even look at the planet. In fact, Marco is self-assured throughout, with eyes closed in smug superiority as he leads Conrad by the hand, helping him over obstacles or pushing him in front of him, or using strange conveyances to transport them—a gondola, a howdah on an elephant's back, or a basket strung between two large beasts. Clearly Marco, like Columbus, is the expedition's leader, though the follower threatens to overtake him at the end with an even larger and more gorgeous letter of his own creation.

But Marco maintains his superiority at least through most of the story. Part of his purpose in maintaining this pose is to prove that he is an uncommon boy, capable of going beyond where other people stop, capable of producing marvelous sights. Marco represents this knowledge as not impossible, for it is merely a question of how far "most" but not "all" other people go. And he uses no magical transport to get himself and Conrad to these marvelous sights. But the alphabet is uncommon and out of the ordinary, and that is his justification for having it. It adds variety and interest to his life. As he says to Conrad, "If you stay home with Zebra / You're stuck in a rut." And this imaginative flight is just the first step in the acquisition of more wisdom:

> *So you see!*
> *There's no end*

To the things you might know,
Depending on how far beyond Zebra you go!

That Conrad invents a new letter beyond the ones that Marco has shown him demonstrates that the imaginative process can go on beyond his own efforts, and that imagination jumps boundaries that are commonly perceived but not really there.

Marco's purpose with these letters is to spell the names of the animals that he sees in his trips. Spelling here seems to have more than one meaning. For the child learning to read and write, spelling is a way to master words and the process of written communication; it demonstrates control and superiority over the words, since knowing how to spell words gives access to them. But in a larger, more mystical sense, spelling is related to casting a spell, which is what Marco has done with Conrad by showing him the animals that he can conjure up because he has access to those new letters. Part of the appeal of these animals is that they are "brand-new" and "wonderful," thus relieving the pedantry and routine of other words. But their other attraction is that they are imaginative and impossible, except as one uses the imagination to find them. Thus, though the book seems to be criticizing traditional school skills of mastering ordinary alphabets and regular spelling, it is also touting the virtues of knowing how to spell, of knowing the correct letters, even if they are self-invented, and of exploring new aspects of the mind to find new answers. By invoking Columbus and by praising the virtues of individuality, Seuss is writing an all-American book, and though its message may make children difficult to control in traditional classrooms, it will also spur them on to higher intellectual performance by encouraging them to go beyond known wisdom to find their own, to find new solutions.

The "List of Letters for People Who Don't Stop at Z" at the end of the book presents a mock catalog and dictionary of those letters that Dr. Seuss has invented and presented in the book. As Bader has said, the letters resemble Oriental pictographs.[11] They are usually combinations of letters—for instance, Wum is a W on top of an M, but the letters are drawn in scripts that are finished with seraphs and other strokes, making them look unusually graceful and always more marvelous than scripts that children are commonly taught to practice their handwriting in. The letters are obviously more complicated not only in their appearance but also in their pronunciation, as they are not simple vowel-consonant combinations, but are sometimes virtually unpronounceable ones, like *Thnad,* or even multisyllabic ones, such as *Fuddle.* The use of the unlikely repeated consonant—double Z's and double K's— makes the letters seem all the more exotic and inventive. And the list of the animals that these letters represent mimics the traditional abecedaria, where animals are usually of the monosyllabic type—C is for *cat.* The reader can refer to this list as a memory device; it unifies an otherwise episodic book and invites the reader into the club of the uncommon imaginers of letters beyond Z—since "Most people stop at the Z." The invitation to name Conrad's gorgeously expansive letter at the end also lures the reader into suggesting other new letters for the alphabet.

The zebra is an appropriate beginning point for Marco's alphabet, since it is an exotic creature, a horse with an otherwise purposeless variation of stripes, done solely for visual effect. The zebra on the cover is strange-looking enough, but Marco's inventions will go beyond even this odd-looking beast. The Z is not a commonly used consonant in English, and so is an appropriate beginning for other letters that are used even less frequently. The zebra on the cover is clearly left behind, as he glances at something that has already whizzed by him; he stands amazed on the surface of an otherwise uninhabited world, which is blue and boring like the world of "most people," but which contrasts sharply to the fuller world of Marco and his alphabet inside the covers.

Some of the letters and animals they represent reappear from other Seuss books—Horton becomes a vehicle for trapping the Sneedle. The Wumbus, a fish that lives on a mountain peak, is the same as the fish from Tibet in *McElligot's Pool.* The fishes that go "Glurk" in the fish book are here the Floob-Boober-Bab-Boober-Bubs. And even the Whos reappear as Itch-a-pods, though not with quite the variety of shapes and sizes as in *Horton Hears a Who!* or *Grinch.* The reappearance of these characters may seem an indication of illustrative inadequacy, with the illustrator unable to imagine a sufficient number of new animals to complete the book. But the more likely explanation is that these characters are readers' favorites from other Seuss books, and welcome the reader back into the same fertile but unpredictable ground found in those earlier books. The fact that such relative unpopulars as Thidwick do not reappear indicates that the author had an accurate gauge on the popularity of his writing.

There are occasional letters that may appeal to an adult's sense of humor—the Quandary, which spends all day worrying whether it is right side up or upside down, the High Gargel-orum, with collars where they gargle, and height like Angelorum, the Latin word for angels. But in the main, the letters and animals are invented to appeal to a child's sense of humor, and to demonstrate for children the richness of language when used imaginatively. For example, *Sneedle* is made to rhyme with *mos-keedle,* and Nutches live in Nitches, which resemble hutches, and force the child through an elaborate set of tongue twisters, demanding both precise reading and precise pronunciation to understand and master the story about them. The book is a demonstration for the message it sends: language is fun, pliable, and adequate for any imaginative flight, especially if one goes beyond the limits posed by common sense.

How the Grinch Stole Christmas!

At the same time he was working on *The Cat in the Hat,* Seuss was expected to produce an annual volume for Random House. One year, he found himself with a deadline but no book for the publisher's Christmas list. The Grinch and his story occurred fortuitously, and the story was written quickly, in a few weeks, except for the last few pages, the resolution of the story. That the story came so easily is tribute to several of its qualities: its archetypal pattern, the author's own feeling of involvement with the Grinch, and the similarity of the Grinch's story to Clement Clark

Moore's "A Visit from St. Nicholas," more popularly known as "The Night before Christmas."

How the Grinch Stole Christmas! is about the Grinch, a dour hater of the Christmas season, who is inspired by the joyous celebration of the Whos in Who-ville to prevent Christmas from coming. He thinks that by stealing all the Christmas decorations, gifts, and food, he will foil the entire community's Christmas spirit. He dresses up as Santa Claus and, with his dog Max dressed as a reindeer, sets out to rob all the homes in Who-ville of their Christmas items. He completely cleans out their homes, leaving behind nothing but bare walls and wires from which the decorations formerly hung. He therefore expects that the Whos will spend the day crying rather than celebrating. When the Grinch finds that they still continue to celebrate by singing their traditional Christmas songs, he is forced to realize that Christmas means more than material things, and that the day and its joy arrive in spite of the absence of material reminders of the season. He is converted to the generous spirit of the Whos, returns their presents and decorations, and on the final page is even shown participating in their traditional Christmas feast.

That the Grinch is something of a caricature of the author is obvious from the author's license plates for his car, "GRINCH," and from one detail about the Grinch in the story: the Grinch has been putting up with the Whos' Christmas celebrations for fifty-three years, presumably all his life, the same age as Seuss was when the book was published. Seuss has shown himself averse to public celebrations, especially of his birthday; he reportedly prefers to spend his birthday in Las Vegas, rather than greet the many schoolchildren who come to his door with songs and cards. His logic is that no one would look for a children's author in a gambling casino.[12] There is a certain good-natured self-abuse here, but the spirit of the Grinch is clearly present in his creator, the sometime recluse who hates noise, merriment, singing, public festivities, and base materialism in any form.

Grinch is clearly an American story, as can be gathered from the Whos' celebration of Christmas. Nowhere does Seuss mention any religious celebration. Instead, he mentions children and toys; large meals of "Who pudding" and roast "Who beast" consumed by the entire community; Christmas songs accompanied by Christmas bells; and all the secular accoutrements that Americans associate with the season: Christmas trees with electric lights; stockings on the mantel, to be stuffed with gifts; Yule logs; wreaths; and "their presents! The ribbons! The wrappings! / The tags! And the tinsel! The trimmings! The Trappings!"[13] In short, the Christmas celebration here is not a spiritual one but is instead one full of things; it is not, however, as the Grinch finds out, empty of spirit. The whole Who culture celebrates the holiday in a fashion typical of such celebrations in the United States, where noncelebrants must make a concerted effort to avoid the season and its promotion by government and commercial enterprises.

So the Grinch's position as a nonparticipant is one that he maintains only by deliberate social isolation. Though he is a Grinch and not a Who, at the end of the book he is welcomed into the Who community. His former isolation was self-imposed. The origin of his attitude toward the holiday is not clear, but the narrator offers several possible explanations:

> It *could* be his head wasn't screwed on just right.
> It *could* be, perhaps, that his shoes were too tight.
> But I think that the most likely reason of all
> May have been that his heart was two sizes too small.

Thus, the explanation may be dementia, or physical discomfort, or even lack of capacity for compassion. The last explanation prevails, since when the Grinch finally converts, the Whos' local legend evolves that his heart at that point grew to adequate size with his conversion.

But his attitude is not uncommon, even in a place where Christmas is celebrated so passionately. Ebenezer Scrooge, though English in origin, has his counterparts in the United States among those who see no reason to rejoice on Christmas. The Grinch's lack of Christmas spirit is echoed by Charlie Brown in the popular televised Christmas special "A Charlie Brown Christmas," and psychologists frequently report that Americans feel depression, at the very season in which negative feeling is hardly allowed, for a variety of reasons: reminiscences of Christmases past that have been less than satisfactory; a feeling of overwork and inadequacy, both emotional and financial; a dread of the rest of the culture, which seems so intent on ignoring bad feelings during the season. One other common feeling is shared by many Americans and the Grinch: Christmas has become commercialized, torn loose from its moral and religious meaning. However, the Grinch's discovery is possible even for the most cynical of noncelebrants, as the message of community feeling and celebration comes through, no matter what happens to sabotage the celebration. "'Maybe Christmas,' he thought, '*doesn't* come from a store. / 'Maybe Christmas . . . perhaps . . . means a little bit more!'"

The possibility that the Grinch's particular dislike for the season may be due to a mental disorder is suggested by the snow-covered cave he lives in on a high hill north of Who-ville. All the details here underscore the coldness and distance of his habitat, and his pink eyes, the only colored detail in several of the pictures of him, make them look bloodshot and particularly misanthropic. But still, the Grinch's feelings are those with which the reader can identify, for they mirror the negative, antisocial envy in all of us. His greatest objection to the season is the noise. The Who children are pictured with loud toys—drums, toy trains, horns, and jack-in-the-boxes. Even the food is loud, as can be seen when the Grinch invades the first Who house, taking every present, including "Pop guns! And Bicycles! Roller skates! Drums! / Checkerboards! Tricycles! Popcorn! And Plums!" The children are pictured playing inside with many of these outside toys, and though the plums are not a particularly noisy fruit, the popcorn, like the pop guns, reminds the reader of the noise that both will make.

The Grinch also objects to the community spirit and bounty evidenced in the Whos' communal Christmas meal. The picture of them dining is a particularly busy one, and the reader can gather that there will be much noise associated with the meal. But as he objected to the "NOISE! NOISE! NOISE! NOISE!" of the toys, so the Grinch objects to the fact that the Whos will "FEAST! /

FEAST! / FEAST! / FEAST! . . . Which was something the Grinch couldn't stand in the least!" It is the fact that the Whos will be doing more than just eating—they will also be enjoying themselves, and overindulging in food—that the Grinch objects to. In similar fashion, he objects to the fact that the Whos will "SING! SING! SING! SING!" again, a protest as much about their feeling of fellowship as about the noise level.

The Grinch thoroughly offends the reader not only by his attitude toward the Whos but also by two unforgivable acts: he abuses his dog, Max, first by making him dress up like a reindeer, with a rack of antlers tied to his head, and then by forcing him to exert all the effort in hauling the large load of stolen Christmas items up the steep height of Mount Crumpit. Max is a loyal, uncomplaining companion, and to force man's best friend to dissemble against his will and to do all the hard work is an unmitigated horror to those who sanctify a dog's friendship.

The second transgression of the Grinch is his lie to Cindy-Lou Who, who is made even more pitiful by her age, "not more than two." She is described as a "tiny Who daughter," making her even more appealing, and the Grinch's lie to her all the more galling. Getting out of bed for a drink of water, she innocently stumbles on the Grinch and asks plaintively, "Santy Claus, why, / *Why* are you taking our Christmas tree? WHY?" It is bad enough that the Grinch has stolen the gifts, but the theft of the tree, that glittery American symbol of Christmas, is the supreme offense.

The Grinch compounds his offense by his reply to Cindy-Lou, which is glib, quickly fabricated, and falsely tender:

"Why, my sweet little tot," the fake Santy Claus lied,
"There's a light on this tree that won't light on one side.
"So I'm taking it home to my workshop, my dear.
"I'll fix it up *there*. Then I'll bring it back *here*."

Cindy-Lou is not wise enough to ask why he does not fix the tree in its place, or why he is in charge of the tree, instead of minding the business of the presents. That the Grinch has taken advantage of her innocence is further compounded by his getting her a drink and sending her back to bed, contented and reassured, to dream more "sweet dreams without care," little suspecting the depth of his treachery.

Though the Grinch dresses up as St. Nick, he is closer to Old Nick, or Satan, in his attitude toward the Whos and Christmas. At one point, the narrator calls him "old liar," when he tells the especially bold lie to Cindy-Lou. Though the lie is later called a "fib," it cannot be so easily diminished in its heinousness. In fact, it is the Grinch's ability to fabricate all sorts of things—lies, reindeer antlers for Max, a Santa Claus suit for himself—that defines his particular brand of demonry. The red in the whites of his eyes burn like demonic fire, and the fact that the Grinch hardly looks like Santa Claus, since his Christmas suit does not cover his tail and the hat does nothing to conceal his pointed ears or vile expression, further suggests his demonic qualities. When the narrator announces that "THE GRINCH / GOT A WONDERFUL, AWFUL IDEA!" to steal all the Christmas trappings from the Whos in order to stop Christmas from coming, he underlines the twisted nature of the Grinch's mind, a mind that can see that a ghastly plot can be wonderful in its profound negativeness.

The Whos make a reappearance here, from *Horton Hears a Who!*, where they were modeled on the Japanese after World War II. Though they clearly no longer represent the Japanese, they are the same remarkably optimistic, hard-working people, who exert themselves as much in their celebrations as they did in their work to rebuild Who-ville in the Horton book. Even Jo-Jo, the little Who whose cry of "Yopp!" saves Who-ville in the earlier book, makes a reappearance, in the tricycle under the Christmas tree, with the tag on it that marks it as his gift. The Whos are still a little people, given to much merrymaking, but they are also unpretentious and forgiving. They celebrate even though the Grinch has stolen all the presents and food, by singing just as lustily as the Grinch anticipated they would before he came up with the idea of the grand theft. The picture of them before and after is exactly the same—a double-page spread of small, buglike people in a variety of shapes, arranged hand in hand in an arch that spans both pages.

The one change is that the background, which before was white, is later red, suggesting the intensity of their singing, in spite of their losses. Their forgiveness of the Grinch is clear when they permit him the honor of carving the roast beast at their meal, this privilege usually going to the host. They defy the Grinch not only by their acceptance of him at their meal, placing him in the position of guest (or host) of honor, but also by their lack of tears at the Grinch's theft. Though the Grinch expects that "their mouths will hang open a minute or two / Then the *Whos* down in *Who*-ville will all cry BOO-HOO!," what happens is quite the opposite:

> But the sound wasn't *sad!*
> Why, this sound sounded *merry!*
> It *couldn't* be so!
> But it WAS merry! VERY!

Though what the Grinch has expected is noise and loud crying, what he gets is music, loud but melodious, as suggested by the musical notes in the picture. While the Whos clearly enjoy the material objects of Christmas, it is the immaterial feeling that prevails.

The moral comes abruptly and with a certain vagueness, the result, perhaps, of the author's difficulty in composing it. For the Grinch, it takes three hours to divine the message of the Whos' celebration. His first realization is that "He HADN'T stopped Christmas from coming! / IT CAME!," indicating the inevitability not only of 25 December arriving each year but also of the celebration that will come with it. After trying to understand this phenomenon for three hours, standing in the snow, the Grinch realizes that "Maybe Christmas . . . *doesn't* come from a store. / Maybe Christmas . . . perhaps . . . means a little bit more!" Exactly what the meaning is is not made clear, but the Grinch then returns the gifts and his heart grows; for the first time in the book he appears in the illustration to be a character associated with Christmas—an elf, though not Santa himself. In the final picture, where he is shown carving the roast, his smile is that of the benign Cat in the Hat and his hands, before menacing and pointy, no longer seem so devious. That he is seated underneath a wreath at the Whos' table nicely rounds out the story pictorially, for the opening page shows a young Who holding the same wreath and looking out at the reader, as though the Who were an illuminated capital from an old manuscript. This same Who with the wreath is shown on the end pages; in fact, the wreath recurs throughout the book as a symbol of the spirit of unity and the attractive festivity of the season. Though the Grinch is not holding this wreath, nor looking through it in the final picture, it emphasizes his change of spirit as it encircles his head like a halo.

Or like a wreath. The comparisons with Moore's "A Visit from St. Nicholas" are mostly at the word level or are implied in the illustration, for, after all, the Grinch is not St. Nick. The Who children of the house that the Grinch first chooses to invade are shown five in a bed, all soundly asleep, like the children who are "nestled all snug in their beds." And though the Who children are not shown dreaming of sugarplums, the Grinch does steal their plums, an unlikely Christmas fruit, though Seuss probably resorted to it because it rhymes with *drums*. However, they are "dreaming sweet dreams without care," dreams not unlike the dreams of sweets in Moore's poem.

The Who mice are stirring, but they do so to reject the pitiful crumbs that the Grinch leaves behind, which are even too small for them. But they are the only inhabitants of Who-ville who are stirring; everyone else is "a-snooze," an antique-sounding word worthy of Moore's miniepic. And for some reason—probably because of the image of the American Santa Claus that Moore initiated and enshrined in his poem—the Grinch insists that he needs a reindeer, needs to climb down the chimney, and needs red, fir-trimmed clothing to impersonate St. Nick. The snowy scene, the evergreens in the landscape, and the cozy, warm houses that the Grinch looks down on, are all reminiscent of the warm home to which St. Nick pays his visit in Moore's poem. Though these borrowings are less direct than the earlier ones, still they show the influence that Moore's poem had on Seuss's attempt to write another Christmas epic, though this time about a spoiler of the season.

The pictures show Seuss at the zenith of his drawing ability.

Three thousand feet up! Up the side of Mt. Crumpit,
He rode with his load to the tiptop to dump it!
"Pooh-Pooh to the *Whos!*" he was grinch-ish-ly humming.
"They're finding out now that no Christmas is coming!
"They're just waking up! I know *just* what they'll do!
"Their mouths will hang open a minute or two
"Then the *Whos* down in *Who*-ville will all cry BOO-HOO!

The pictures are more complex, with more background and detail than in *The Cat in the Hat,* but there is the sameness in the grins of the Grinch and the Cat when both are at the height of their powers, committing lies, overstatements, and other forms of mayhem. In *Grinch,* the lines are sure and dark, and the use of color simple—only red and shades of it color the pages, though a contrasting Christmas green appears on the front cover. The Whos, though ethnically similar, are given a surprising array of differing appearances, and in spite of their smallness, they manage to fill up the two-page spreads quite adequately.

In fact, the two-page spreads are used to their maximum potential here, with the movement from upper left to lower right, and from lower left to upper right, emphasizing distance, both vertically and horizontally. For example, the height of Mount Crumpit, from which the Grinch threatens to dump the Christmas gifts, is accented by the depth of its base, in the lower left-hand corner of the left page, beginning in the outskirts of Who-ville, and by its rising upward and leftward across the two pages. The precariousness of the sleigh, almost ready to fall over the sheer cliff face, is emphasized not only by the sleigh's perch on the edge of the cliff but also by the gifts already dangling over the edge; the precariousness is further emphasized by a passing bird, one of Seuss's silent commentators on the action, looking up in anxiety from below the dangling articles. The large size of the page allows even small details much more emphasis than do the smaller pages of the Beginner Books, and these details—for example, in the picture of Mt. Crumpit, the still-pink eyes of the Grinch and the little bird—demand that the viewer pay close attention to the entire picture, rather than just take in the picture at one glance. For example, when the Grinch steals the Whos' food, leaving only crumbs too small even for a mouse, the mouse is a small detail in the larger picture of the empty room, with only bare walls, bare mantle, and the Grinch's hands stealing the last remaining item of Christmas, the log from the fire. The focus in the picture is clearly on the Grinch's hands and sleeves, the only colored detail in the picture. But the mouse appears just below the last words on the right-hand page, and becomes apparent to the reader/

viewer only as the eye continues to move to the right and downward. But this one detail stops the reader from turning the page; the reader sees the mouse, with his disdain for the crumb, and stops, most likely lingering even longer to reexamine the entire picture. Among these small details, the pink of the Grinch's eyes is particularly compelling, especially since the close-up portraits of the Grinch fill nearly a whole page, and the only detail in color is the pink of the eyes. But stopping to look at the eyes allows the viewer the pause necessary to reexamine the other details of the Grinch—sinuous, pointy fingers; malevolent grin—that further define him.

The consistency of the fantasy of the Whos who live in Whoville is apparent in these details. The Whos' refrigerator is made by General Who-Lectric, as emblazoned on the door, and the Grinch is careful to steal canned goods, which the text tells us are *Who*-hash. The first house that the Grinch steals from is the home of J. P. Who, as the sign says over the door, and the gifts under the tree include a red wagon, with the brand name Who Express, and two wrapped gifts tagged For Uncle Who and For Auntie Who. Though the parallels between the Whos and Americans is clear, Seuss does not borrow without transforming items into consistent Who details.

The language is equally full of details. The thread with which the Grinch fastens on Max's reindeer antlers is particularly noted as "red," and the number of sizes that the Grinch's heart is too small is exactly "two," though it grows "three sizes" larger as he converts, indicating that his conversion is not simply adequate, it is abundant. For "three hours," he thinks about the persistence of the Whos' celebration, despite their lack of presents, contemplating the "puzzle" not with his head or his mind but with his "puzzler." Even the placement of a particular word in a line makes the action clearer. For example, when the Grinch decides to steal the Christmas tree, he says, "I will stuff *up* the tree!," not that he will stuff the tree up the chimney. The placement of the word *up* emphasizes, with extraordinary economy, the exertion of the Grinch in pushing everything uphill, especially through the tight opening of the chimney.

There are times when Seuss exploits the rhyme to give the text a childlike simplicity. *Nimbly* rhymes with *chimbley,* a child's mispronunciation, and *houses* rhymes with *mouses,* a typical child's misconstructed plural. The occasional oversized capital, and the occasional word printed in red, give the text a sort of antique quality. And the use of italics and full capitalization make the accent of the verse easy to follow.

That a classic Christmas story should have come from the pen of a nonparticipant in the celebration is ironic, but that it should have been enshrined by a television version of the book is not. After all, Seuss had experience with film during his military service under Frank Capra, and had won two Academy Awards for his work after the war. It is a short jump from film to television, one that Seuss made easily in the television adaptation of this book. The author maintained artistic control over the production, further assuring its consistency and quality. The television version included songs not contained in the book and featured Boris Karloff as the narrator. Seuss has particularly praised Karloff for the attention he gave to the script: "He took the script and studied it for a week as if it were Shakespeare. He figured out all the nuances. That's one of the reasons why it works so well."[14] With such careful attention to the language, such a well-known author, and such an all-American theme, it is not surprising that the book and the television version have both become classics in such a short time—less than thirty years. In 1971 Seuss won the Peabody Award for this television special. Though the book was not a success of the same magnitude as *The Cat in the Hat,* it still continues to sell, especially at Christmas time, and its sales are at least partly encouraged by the yearly rebroadcast of the television version.

4

The Beginnings of the Empire:
The Cat in the Hat
and Its Legacy

The Cat in the Hat is the book that made Dr. Seuss famous. Without *The Cat,* Seuss would have remained a minor light in the history of children's literature. With it, he introduced himself into the public schools in the United States, where generations of readers have learned about him who otherwise would not have. With the series of Beginner Books that *The Cat* inaugurated, Seuss promoted both his name and the cause of elementary literacy in the United States.

The Cat in the Hat

The first Beginner Book was universally well received by critics at the time of its first issue, and few voices have criticized it since, except the minority who point to the Cat's essentially anarchic behavior and the writer's apparent approval of it. But the vast preponderance of critics have praised the book for its story line, which remains interesting despite the carefully controlled vocabulary; for its robust use of verse; and for its vivid, even brash, illustration.

The story begins with Sally and her unnamed brother, the narrator of the story, lamenting a dreary day to be spent inside the house doing nothing. (Oddly enough, Sally is the name of the younger sister of Dick and Jane, characters in a notoriously bad series of primers—was Seuss poking fun?) They cannot figure out for themselves how to keep occupied, when the Cat arrives unannounced and proposes to show the children some amusing games.

The Cat then creates mayhem, first by a game he called "UP-UP-UP with a Fish,"[1] wherein he balances on a ball, while handling not only the pet fish but several other objects, until he falls, along with all the objects. He then brings in two little monsters called Thing One and Thing Two, who insist on flying kites indoors. After the Things have thoroughly demolished what little order is left in the house, the fish spies the children's returning mother. The brother catches the Things with a net and orders the Cat to remove them and to take himself with them. The mess remains until the Cat fortuitously returns with a magic machine to clean up, just in time. The reader is left with the closing rhetorical question of whether the children should tell their mother about what has gone on.

John Hersey and the Inspiration to Write.
Even a brief plot summary demonstrates that *The Cat* contrasts markedly with the quality of the basal readers of the 1950s. In fact, it was the paucity of interesting reading and good illustration in the primers that inspired John Hersey to comment in a 1954 article in *Life* magazine that Seuss might well try his hand at a primer. Hersey, like many others before him in the history of American education, lamented the fact that so few children in American public schools of the time were learning to read competently. He pointed a finger not so much at educators but rather at the poor quality of the reading material that was being presented to young readers at the time. He claimed that children felt that their intelligence was insulted by such boring, unchallenging reading, and that the pursuit of reading was hardly honored by such palid, pastel, middle-class illustration as was common in those books.[2]

The comment that Dr. Seuss should write a primer was not directed to Seuss at any great length. It was simply an offhand remark at the end of a paragraph, suggesting a number of illustrators who might well succeed in the genre of the primer. "Why should they not have pictures that widen rather than narrow the associative richness the children give to the words they illustrate—drawings like those wonderfully imaginative genius among children's illustrators, Tenniel, Howard Pyle, 'Dr. Seuss,' Walt Disney?"[3] It is noteworthy that Hersey did not single out Seuss for his use of language or presumed ability to compose with a limited vocabulary. But Seuss's use of language in *The Cat in the Hat* makes the book remarkable. The success of the story, despite a total vocabulary of only 237 different words, establishes the book's claim to fame more so than the illustrations, which vary little from what readers of Seuss had come to expect. With Hersey's offhand suggestion, Seuss took up the challenge, thinking that writing a book with a limited vocabulary would take him only a few weeks at most. Much to his surprise, writing the book took him over a year.

The task began with the limited vocabulary list for primers from the textbook division of Houghton Mifflin, with Seuss inventing possible story lines. Though Seuss still composes Beginner Books, he no longer limits his use of vocabulary as severely as he did in this first of the series. *The Cat* proved his point that limited vocabulary challenges rather than restrains the skillful writer. The confines of the vocabulary did present certain problems: for instance, the lack of complementary, or opposite, words, and words that had some adventurous suggestiveness to him. Sometimes his ideas took him in directions that required vocabulary not on the list, though the words were ones that children clearly would recognize with a little prompting from the context. After a lengthy period of frustration, Seuss looked for the first two words on a given list that rhymed: *cat* and *hat*.[4] Thus the story was off and running. The author still found himself writing and rewriting in order to keep the narrative down to its essentials, to meet the demands of the limited vocabulary.

The opening lines of the book are flat, like much other Seuss language labeled as deadpan by one critic.[5] Certainly "The sun did not shine" does not sound like the beginning of a book that

has become a classic. But the consequent rhyme and repetition of
words in the last line of the first page indicate that this is not
ordinary language. "So we sat in the house / All that cold, cold,
wet day." The opening conforms to Seuss's stated goal that "it is
important to open with a familiar word" to encourage the reader
to read by not stymieing him with difficulty, and "so that the
reader, recognizing it, can sound out similar words."[6] The "similar" word here is *sat,* which rhymes with *cat* and *hat,* and has the
same vowel sound as *Sally.*

Neither the language nor the situation presage an eventful
book, for the opening picture shows Sally and her brother gazing,
with hardly any expression, through the window out onto the
"cold, cold, wet day." A bird in a nearby tree stands as mute tes-
timony to the inclement weather, as he grimaces when a raindrop
hits him on the head. Going outside to play is out of the question.
The second page shows what the children had planned to do: a
bicycle, a tennis racket and ball, and a large beachball are pictured as motionless comment on the foiled plans. As the narrator
says, it is "Too wet to go out / And too cold to play ball."

In his article, Hersey lamented the characterization in primers
of "abnormally courteous, unnaturally clean boys and girls."[7] The
Cat and his friends are nothing if not an antidote to this sort of
character. What courtesy there is simply covers over the Cat's
purpose to make a mess while having fun. The anxiety created in
the children over his behavior is accompanied by the reader's enjoyment of the chaos resulting from the Cat's reckless abandon-
ment in his pleasures.

The Children.
Throughout the book, the problem confronting the children is
what to do to occupy themselves. Even when the Cat is in the
house making mischief, the children do not know what to do,
either to get him to leave or to stop his foolishness. The statement, "We did nothing at all," holds for nearly the entire book—
in fact, the only action of the children is to catch the Things and
order the Cat and his pets out of the house. For the rest of the
story they are innocent bystanders, nearly mute observers of

what goes on. The problem comes to a head with the Things. The fish urges the children: "So, as fast as you can, / Think of something to do!" about them. The children are consistently pictured in the corners of the two-page spreads, looking on with astonished, but otherwise inactive, amazement. This separation of the children from the main action of the story allows the child reader to participate in the fun of the anarchy and upset without becoming a guilty participant in the mess that results. Still, the children in the story are not without involvement; when their mother's arrival is imminent, the fish asks them, "what will she do to us?" Certainly their mother will not hold them blameless. They will be responsible for cleaning up the mess, even if they did not make it themselves. Thus, the children in the book are motivated by anxiety, which is not transferred to the child reader, who is free to enjoy the mess.

The Mother.
It is clear to the reader at the end, when the boy narrator asks, "what would YOU do" about the mother's questions, that keeping quiet is the answer. First of all, the children's lack of participation in the actual mayhem does not clear them of the guilt of having countenanced it. Nor does it absolve them of the crime of having admitted a stranger into the house in the absence of the parent, especially since they have been amply warned by the fish to keep the Cat out. Furthermore, it is not clear whether this mother, who, the fish implies, is a lover of order and cleanliness, would believe the story of the improbable Cat's ruckus, given the present neatness of the house and the children's presence in the seats by the window as she enters, the same place that they were seated when the story opened and the same place that the mother would presume they have remained throughout. Though the final question is presented rhetorically and does not demand a response, the likely answer from a child's perspective is that the children had better simply leave their mother in the dark and give a child's typical answer to the question, "What did you do all day?" "Nothing."

The mother's status as a realist and literalist is underscored by

Seuss's method of illustrating her: her face is never seen; we only see her foot entering into view through the window as the children realize she is about to return, and her hand appearing as she reenters through the door. Furthermore, her foot wears a no-nonsense shoe, neatly tied, shown in a full, forthright stride. Her hand is also noteworthy. Frequently, Seuss resorts to using the illustrational shorthand of comic books and gives characters only three of four digits. The Cat and the Things have thumbs but only two or three fingers; mother, however, has all her fingers and one clearly illustrated thumb protruding through the doorway. There is no fantasy about Seuss's illustration of her. She is fully human, realistically portrayed, in contrast to those characters of fantasy, the Cat, the talking fish, and the Things.

But the fantasy book declines to provide the answer to the realist mother's final question. Once again, the children are inactive and indecisive. Throughout the book the narrator reports that the children "did not know what to say" or "did not know what to do." All that they can imagine for themselves is either outdoor play or passive reflection on the Cat's visit after he leaves. Sometimes it is simply speechlessness that renders them actionless, as when the Things introduce themselves.

> And Sally and I
> Did not know what to do.
> So we had to shake hands
> With Thing One and Thing Two.

But the experience of the book itself provides an answer to the quest to find something to do: if one is stuck indoors at home on a rainy day, one can always read and enjoy the action vicariously.

The Cat.
The Cat's avowed goal is to give the children "fun that is funny." The distinction between ordinary fun and "fun that is funny" is one clear to children—there is the kind of fun to which children are sentenced by their elders, which is serious, in that children learn real lessons from their play. And there is the kind of fun that is hilarious. The problem for the children in the book is that

"it is fun to have fun but you have to know how," as the Cat says. These children need a lesson in how to be interesting to themselves. As Mary Lystad has pointed out, the book celebrates the creative use of leisure and answers the human need for play and adventure. "The message is clear—if the world is bleak, change it, create a new world!"[8]

The book encourages this use of fantasy, even if the children are warned by the fish against participating in it. Certainly no harm comes to children who read about this fantasy as long as they do not seek to re-create it themselves. The fact that the story takes place at home—the same place the book can be read—reassures the child that an interesting story can take place within familiar confines—and that the experience of reading at home can be interesting as well. Adventure need not require actual physical departure from the locus of safety and security.

Though the story includes intrusion into and catastrophe within this locus, the children and the Cat always behave courteously to each other. In fact, this courtesy serves as verbal camouflage for the Cat's real intent. He promises that his "tricks are not bad," but in the end they are labeled as "bad tricks" by the boy narrator. They are good tricks only in the sense that they exhibit an uncommon propensity to create anarchy—in other words, the tricks are particularly proficient in their trickery. The problem is that the Cat's statement that "my tricks are not bad" is evasive. The statement does not necessarily imply that the tricks are good in the sense that the mother would talk about "good tricks" or "good fun"—that they are appropriate indoor play for well-behaved children. The tricks are also not "good" in that the Cat executes them poorly—he falls off the ball in his balancing game and fails to show that his Things are, as he claims, "tame" and therefore fit playfellows.

His one good trick is his return with his marvelous machine to clean up. He baldly asserts, as if he were a model child, that "I always pick up all my playthings." But it is not his love of orderliness that prevails here. Until he is thrown out of the house, he gives no heed to the mess he has created. Nor is it his desire to be obedient and well behaved. The whole book has depended on the premise that the Cat is careless of what the children's mother

Then our mother came in
And she said to us two,
"Did you have any fun?
Tell me.   What did you do?"

And Sally and I did not know
What to say.
Should we tell her
The things that went on there that day?

Should we tell her about it?

Now, what SHOULD we do?

Well . . .

What would YOU do

If your mother asked YOU?

would wish. His return is motivated mostly by his desire to show off with his new marvel. It performs the impossible by cleaning up everything, even though the fish has elsewhere pointed out that the mess is so extensive, "We can not pick it up. / There is no way at all!" Luckily, both fish and children are rescued by the exhibitionist Cat and his machine.

Furthermore, as the book's few detractors have pointed out, the fact that the Cat cleans up does not really undo his initial action of having performed the "bad tricks" in the first place. He and the children have avoided the children's mother's criticism, but truth to tell, he should not have come to the house and should not have done his bad tricks. But fortunately, the book is not concerned with the didactic intent of teaching children to play appropriately indoors. It is meant to entertain, and certainly the chaos that the Cat brings into the house is more interesting and entertaining for the child reader than any more orderly pursuits that the day might otherwise have suggested.

The Fish.
The opposition of the fish and the Cat creates the tension in the story. Otherwise, the narrative would proceed with the Cat making trouble but with the possibility that the reader would have no concern for the children or the mother. The Cat and the fish are linked in combat both by the incompatibility of their species and by the language used to describe them. The Cat's formal name is "The Cat in the Hat," the proper name indicated by the use of the capital letters. The fish, after he falls out of his bowl when the Cat drops him in the balancing game, is referred to as the "fish in the pot." The two full names are even juxtaposed in two consecutive lines. The opposition of the two animals is exacerbated by the Cat's courteous, but nevertheless patronizing, reassurance to the fish: "Have no fear, little fish," a tone of voice guaranteed to insult.

That the fish represents the mother is made clear not only by his concern for what she would say if she saw the mayhem the Cat is perpetrating but also by the fish's use of the word *should*— "He should not be here / When your mother is out"—echoing the kind of language that parents use when issuing orders to their children. But the fish does not remain aloof from the children and their plight. The text does not offer the possibility that the fish will distance himself from the calamity around him by telling the mother that he warned the children and had no part in the action. Instead, the children claim him as a member of the family. He is "our fish," and though he at first tells the children about what "your mother" would want, at the end of the book, he calls her "our mother," and wonders what she will do and say to "us."

The fish's complicity in the action is underscored by his presence in the second picture of the book, showing the children sitting by the window, with him in his fishbowl asleep. Like the children, he, too, is bored. In the final picture, his knowing look at the reader contrasts with the children's wide-eyed speechlessness at their mother's question about what they did all day. The fish makes eye contact with the reader and assures him that something did go on but that silence is the better part of valor in this case. He has succeeded in sparing the children, the reader, and himself, as well, from the difficulties of telling a mother that something fantastic and not altogether to her liking occurred.

The character of the boy narrator is rescued from criticism by his gradual taking on of the fish's point of view. It is not until his mother is clearly visible through the window on her way home that the boy is finally roused to speech and to action. But the narrator is not convinced to take this action simply by the fish's warning about the Things. In fact, he initially greets them quite courteously, agreeing to shake hands with them.

The Things.
However, when it becomes clear that the Things are not "tame," as the Cat claims, the boy must take action. The exact nature of the Things is not clear—they look peculiarly like children in red pajamas, yet their designation as Things indicates that they are not human, though what their exact species is not known. Clearly they are petlike creatures, kept in a box and described as "tame" by the Cat, as domesticated wild creatures might be described. The Cat also gives them a "pat," as one would furry pets. But the Things are not really so tame. They choose, after the initial demonstration of their training in the proffered handshakes, to fly

kites in the house, an activity clearly prohibited to well-behaved children. The narrator seems to be describing some kind of wild animal or monster when he describes their game.

> Then those Things ran about
> With big bumps, jumps and kicks
> And with hops and big thumps
> And all kinds of tricks.

Like things that go bump in the night are these Things, who do not know how to play as proper guests or pets should. Thus, it seems particularly appropriate that the only way to capture them is by using a butterfly net. The turning point comes when the Things make those uncivilized noises.

Reading Readiness—Preparing the Reader to Read.
The Cat in the Hat teaches children many lessons about books. As Seuss has said, children may spend much of first grade learning two fundamental lessons about books: first, that a book is not simply a "colorful object," and second, that there is some kind of correspondence between the words on the page and the illustrations.[9] As to the first lesson, in no case in the story itself are books shown as toys, though they are common household items, since the Cat finds two of them to balance in his unsuccessful game.

As to the second point, the text is clearly set off from the illustration on the page, and is not easily confused as part of the illustration, a frequent problem for children who do not yet recognize the convention of words and text on the same page. The text is always to one side of the page, with the illustration taking up the rest of the space. The lines of poetry are usually placed below the illustration. The limited vocabulary—starting out with simple language and proceeding to build on the knowledge of that simple vocabulary with rhyme words that are similar, but not the same—encourages the child's sense of mastery of the language and his ability to continue with the story, without being stopped by unfamiliar words. There is only one illustration per two-page spread, and nothing appears in the text that is not also presented in the illustration. Thus, if the child has problems with a particular word, the context of the illustration may help him to identify it. Occasionally a word may identify an item that the child might not recognize in the illustration.

The way Dr. Seuss uses the space on the page further encourages the child to read. His announced intention to encourage the child to read on by creating a "cliff-hanger" effect on each right-hand page[10] is particularly well demonstrated in *The Cat in the Hat*. Sounds appear in the illustration, such as the *BUMP!* that announces the Cat's arrival, on the right-hand page, appearing to emanate from even farther to the right, off the right-hand side of the right page. The illustrated *BUMP!* has letters that are gradually shaded, from bottom to top, further indicating directionality and leading the viewer's eye off the edge of the right page.

In another instance, when the Cat plays the balancing game, the text narrating his action appears on the left page. But the ellipses that end the pages on which the game is described indicate that more fun will follow on the next double-page spread. The use of this punctuation underscores the contents of the lines. "'But that is not ALL I can do!' / Said the Cat. . ." and "But that is not all! / Oh, no. / That is not all. . . ." As the Cat becomes involved with balancing more objects, he lists and leans more precariously to the right. Whereas he starts off fairly erect on the ball as he begins the game, he deviates from this uprightness by the list of his body, the outstretched limbs and tail, and the gradual sliding of his hat to the left of his head, or as the viewer sees it, to the right of the page. The general rightward motion of the line in this progression of pictures, and the addition of the objects and their complication of the visual effect, all aid in underscoring the language's effect of inducing the reader to move on by turning the page, by proceeding farther right in the story toward further complication and final resolution. The frequent use of questions to end the text on a particular page—"Why do you sit there like that?" and "Would you like to shake hands / With Thing One and Thing Two?"—is another method of creating that cliff-hanger effect. At the end of the story, the device is so effective that some readers may decide to turn the page in order to find the answer to the final line in the book, "What would YOU do / If your mother asked YOU?"

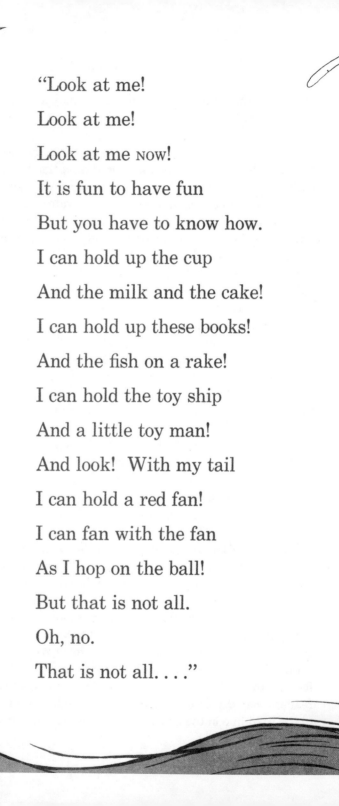

"Look at me!
Look at me!
Look at me NOW!
It is fun to have fun
But you have to know how.
I can hold up the cup
And the milk and the cake!
I can hold up these books!
And the fish on a rake!
I can hold the toy ship
And a little toy man!
And look! With my tail
I can hold a red fan!
I can fan with the fan
As I hop on the ball!
But that is not all.
Oh, no.
That is not all. . . ."

Dr. Seuss also aids the reader by frequently using full capitalization for a word to indicate emphasis, further marking the stresses in the poetic meter. The lilt of the anapestic tetrameter, much like that of a Strauss waltz, also carries the reader along, establishing a pace for the language and a rhythm to the book, a movement further underscored by the use of the two-page spread for each illustration.

The use of verse permits the author to reinforce new words by repeating them. However, a writer of children's books is to make sure the device of repetition is used to reinforce the words, not simply used gratuitously; the story must call forth the repetition, a feat which Seuss has carried off admirably, especially in his use of the Cat's cleanup machine. The device of the machine allows the narrator to recall all the things the Cat has scattered around throughout the story as the machine picks them up. Thus, at the end, all the new vocabulary that has been introduced is brought together and repeated. The shortened line length makes the rhyme more obvious, thus making the reading even easier.

The rhyme also permits the reader to find a clue for the pronunciation of a new word, or an ambiguous word, in the word with which it must rhyme. In two instances, Seuss uses this capacity of rhyme particularly astutely. In the first case, he cues the reader about the pronunciation of *head* by forcing it to rhyme with *said*. Though the two are not sight rhymes, the clue to the less obviously pronounced word is clear from the more familiar word. In the second case, the author clues the reader in to the proper pronunciation of *bow* by indicating that it rhymes with *now* and not *no*. With the device of rhyme, the author avoids many problems of introducing unfamiliar vocabulary, and shows the reader one of the mysteries of language: that with a simple change of a consonant, the entire meaning of a word changes.

There are other aspects of handling books that children learn from reading *The Cat*. The use of opening and closing quotation marks to indicate dialogue, the use of exclamation points and question marks to indicate cadence of language, even the numbering of pages (though not all of the pages are numbered here, since numerals would sometimes interfere with the artwork) all teach about the progression of story and familiarize children with the various indicators in the text and on the page of how to use a book in order to get it to render its story.

Furthermore, the child learns, despite the simplified vocabulary, that the language of conversation, as he hears it all day, is not like the language of books. Here, the principal difference is the use of anapestic tetrameter verse, though there are other differences: for example, archaic language, such as "have no fear" (as opposed to "don't be afraid,") and "gown" for what is clearly a simple dress; and archaic uses for familiar words, such as "lit" to mean touched down onto a surface, rather than having been set on fire. Consistent with what is known about children's language acquisition and their early inability to understand negations embedded in contractions—"don't" frequently does not register, though "no" is always clear—Seuss does not use contractions, and this lack of contractions gives the language a formal quality; the fish asserts that "I do NOT wish to fall" rather than the more conversational expression of the same wish, "I don't want to fall."

Above all, Seuss sticks to his principle of simplified vocabulary, not mentioning any word in the text that a child would not be able to read. The Cat in the Hat, consistent with his gentlemanly facade, carries an umbrella, which forms part of his costume as surely as his hat. But *umbrella* is not the kind of word likely to show up on a primer vocabulary list. Thus, it is never mentioned in the text but is simply a part of the visual commentary and complement that the illustration forms around the text.

Seuss's use of language is particularly precise; the milk that the Cat balances is not "in a dish" but "on a dish." Rather than resort to the common phrase "a book in one hand," Seuss describes the Cat's action more precisely with the phrase "a book on one hand," which not only is more accurate but also underscores the precariousness of the Cat's grip. He does not grasp the book in his hand but balances it less firmly on his finger. Seuss also investigates and plays with certain common collocations, such as "fell down," a redundancy without a clear indication of where "up" is from which the falling takes place. But this is one of the peculiarities of common speech that Seuss plays with. When the Cat "fell on his head," the thought is completed with the lines, "He came down with a bump / From up there on the ball."

Seuss also investigates, through the device of polyptoton, the various grammatical uses of a word,[11] as with the word *fan,* which can be both noun and verb. The Cat indicates that "With my tail / I can hold a red fan!" showing that the fan is a noun, but he and Seuss further play with the word and the object in the next line, "I can fan with the fan," showing that the word has more than one grammatical function. Even the line "It is fun to have fun" investigates the two slightly different meanings of the word fun: having fun and funniness are not quite the same thing. Thus, Seuss introduces the child reader into the playfulness that language can have when it is tinkered with, and sanctions this playfulness by his expert use of it.

Children also learn about the nature of stories. *The Cat* has a typical story's shape—a beginning, middle, and end. To end the story efficiently, Dr. Seuss allows a one-page resolution of the problems of the day with the Cat's cleanup machine. Seuss gives the child reader a closed ending, with all the loose ends tied up, and it is a happy ending; in fact, the child reader will probably find this particular ending triumphant. The Cat has cleaned up for the children and has provided them with a full day's entertainment and excitement, and yet the situation allows them to remain silent to their mother about what has gone on. The ending is yet another "good trick," this time on their mother.

Illustration.
Of all the devices Seuss uses in the book to encourage reading and the mastery of stories, the most obvious and most effective is illustration. The pictures are full of the detail specified by the text without being so busy that the specificity is distracting. The simplified backgrounds keep the focus clearly on the objects described in the text, and the gradual accumulation of detail keeps the number of objects from overwhelming. Seuss provides further indicators of how to interpret the illustrations by the various facial expressions, especially those of the children. They are seldom the main subjects of illustration, and yet they are always present. Their expressions direct the eye and the attitude toward the main

subject, thus drawing the viewer further into emotional involvement with both illustration and story. The fish as commentator, both in the text and in his illustrated expression, gives another point of view on the action. When the fish asks, "Do I like this?" the reader can both read the answer in the text and see his expression in the illustration, which clearly features the fish's face. The various splashes of water and the motion lines, indicating exasperation or worry, accentuate the pictures and provide further clues to the fish's evaluation of the situation. Though the pictures appear simple, they are full of complex clues available to the beginning reader.

The pictures are colorful, exploiting a new technique in offset lithography developed at the time. For all the perceived variety of color, there are really only four colors used, albeit in varying shades and tones: the white of the page, the black of the printing and outlines, the red of the Cat's hat, which fades to degrees of pink, and the various depths of blue. It is Seuss's ability to fool the eye into thinking that there are more colors present that is particularly remarkable.

Overall, Seuss broke new ground here, forcing past the limits of vocabulary, printing convention, printing technology, and illustration, showing that the limited-vocabulary book's capabilities had not been fully explored by textbook companies. He also set a benchmark for excellence in characterization and plot for writers who followed, both in the Random House Beginner Book series and in other easy-reader series.

The Cat in the Hat Comes Back

Unfortunately, Seuss was unable to equal this high standard in the sequel to *The Cat in the Hat,* though the second book is hardly a failure. With the obvious success of *The Cat,* both in commercial and educational circles, and the establishment of the Beginner Books division of Random House, the demand was on for another Seuss book for the series. The sequel was designed not only to ride the success of the first book to further commercial success but also to prove that the first book was not a fluke, that the limited-vocabulary book had more than one story to it. If *The Cat in the Hat Comes Back* had been the first, rather than the second, Beginner Book, its merits would be much more obvious: interesting characters; an interesting, cumulatively naughty story that allows the child reader to indulge himself in pleasure; and vibrant illustrations that exploit the limits of the page.

The story opens with weather even more inimical to childhood leisure than *The Cat*. In the aftermath of a snow storm, Sally and her brother have been ordered to clear walkways in the snow by their mother, who once again has left for the day. The Cat in the Hat reappears, this time on skiis, and barges into the house. The boy pursues him and finds him in the bath. The Cat's primary offense is eating a cake, complete with pink frosting, in the tub. The boy orders the Cat out of the tub and the house. But when the water drains, it is clear that the Cat has left a pink ring in the tub, which he proceeds to remove with mother's dress. He removes the stain from the dress to the wall, to the children's father's shoes, to a hall runner, to the bedspread.

But the bedspread presents a problem, and he calls forth helpers, who reside under his hat and answer the question as to why the Cat wears such a preposterous hat: it is the home of little helper cats A, B, C, and so on. The helpers remove the pink stain from the bed, with milk, which they put into a pan, and then blow out the door with a fan. But this action stains the snow outside. Little cats D, E, F, and so on, are called forth, with the sole purpose to spread the stain until it envelops the whole yard. It is little cat Z, with a secret cleaning aid called Voom, who magically cleans up the world, including the pathways to the door. Finally he blows himself and all the other little cats back into the big Cat's hat. The big Cat blithely walks out of the story with an offer to return, with all the little cats, should the children ever require spot removal again.

Characterization.
The characters are consistent with those developed in the earlier book. Though the fish does not reappear, Sally and her brother have learned their lesson about the dangerous complications that the Cat's most innocent actions can yield in their lives. Sally has

only to remind her brother once: "You know what he did / The last time he was here."[12] With this prompting, the boy narrator takes over management of the Cat. But it is impossible to avoid involvement with the Cat, since he infectiously initiates conversation and invites himself into the house before the children can bar him, either physically or verbally. Thus begins the complication of the action.

The boy narrator must deal with the Cat because by the time the boy reaches the house, the Cat is already in the tub eating the cake. But this time the boy is not hesitant; he labels the Cat's bath for what it is. "What a bad thing to do!" When the Cat prevaricates, the boy takes action. "You get out of this house! / We don't want you about!" But the Cat stays around long enough to deal with the "pink cat ring" in the tub. His ability to deal with the complications makes him indispensable. Once again, he exhibits the overreaching optimism about his abilities. Even up to the point when he cleans the spot off the rug onto the bed, he is sure that he knows how to deal with the situation. "It is good that your dad / Has the right kind of bed," he confidently asserts, though he later discovers, on closer examination, "This is NOT the right kind of a bed."

But even this complication does not make the situation impossible; the task may be "hard," as even the Cat admits, but all he needs is help. "I can't do it alone." He knows who to summon, calling forth the first three cats to get the spot off the bed and out of the house. He then calls on cats D through Y to scatter it throughout the yard. Finally, the pink color envelops the whole double-page spread of the book. But the Cat knows that scattering it is necessary, so that he can call forth little cat Z with the Voom. Once again, he justifies his self-confidence in spite of the mess he creates in the process of finding the ultimate solution.

And once again, the children become bystanders, though this time not because of their own inaction but because the Cat beats them to it. As soon as the Cat begins, the rest of the action, including the resolution, depends on him and his helpers. This time, the children know that their mother will blame them if they leave the mess behind. But this time, the children are responsible not only for the inside of the house but also for the outside—almost all outdoors, as implied by their mother's nonspecific order to "Clean all this away." It is as though Seuss and their mother have put them in charge of the whole ecosystem. The pink stain on the snow would be particularly obvious to their mother, but it is not clear that it is harmful. On the other hand, it is not clean by their mother's definition, and so it must go. The pink stain looks peculiarly like a pink version of Oobleck from the earlier Bartholomew book; it is sticky and prone to spreading. The stain looks back to an earlier Seuss book and forward to a later one: *The Lorax,* where there are characters who are responsible for environmental preservation. Fortunately for the beginning reader, *The Cat in the Hat Comes Back* is not the same kind of morality story that *Bartholomew and the Oobleck* and *The Lorax* are; rather, it is an entertaining, humorous story, made mostly for fun.

Occasionally Sally takes on the mother's role here, with speech that sounds peremptory and proscriptive. She warns her brother—"Don't you talk to that cat. . . / You know what he did the last time he was here"—with a sort of smug "I told you so" attitude. Though she and her brother take immediate action in this book to keep the same cataclysm from recurring, the Cat drags them into it. His glib reassurance, like that of a bossy houseguest, starts the trouble. "Keep your mind on your work. / You just stay there, you two. I will go in the house / And find something to do." His plea that "I just want to go in / To get out of the snow" appeals to any host's sense of hospitality for the less fortunate in bad weather. But the damage is done because he moves so fast, wearing skiis with bells on the front, which propel him into the house more quickly than the boy running up the hill can move. The boy narrator is more active than in the earlier story, immediately ordering the Cat out of the house, with no thought for etiquette. "You get out of this house! / We don't want you about!" Unfortunately, the Cat has already started the story in motion by his pink ring around the tub.

Language.
Like the magic machine that cleans up at the end of *The Cat in the Hat,* Voom and its workings are equally mysterious, though

its application on the pink snow is clearly appropriate, according to the narrator.

> Now, don't ask me what Voom is.
> I never will know.
> But, boy! let me tell you
> It DOES clean up snow!

Voom's actions are almost beyond words, except the multiple utterance of its own name, in various grammatical usages, to describe it. "Then the Voom . . . / It went VOOM! / And, oh boy! What a VOOM!" This made-up word is uncharacteristic of *The Cat in the Hat* and illustrates an unusual instance in a Beginner Book of a lack of vocabulary to cover the action adequately. It is also a minor deviation from the prescribed lists of limited vocabulary used in the earlier book. But it also indicates the fun with language made possible by multiple usages of one word. Dr. Seuss had already proven with the earlier book that the limited vocabulary could be used successfully, so perhaps the deviation from word lists was acceptable.

The fact that the book otherwise adheres to a traditional form, the abecedaria, perhaps mitigates the obvious transgression of commonly accepted educational practice: that children should be taught useful vocabulary. *Voom* is not a dictionary word. The relaxation of the high educational standards of the first Cat book are obvious elsewhere. The vocabulary in *The Cat Comes Back* is much more conversational than in the earlier book, with contractions, such as "don't" and "can't," and certain childlike exclamations—"Oh, boy!" for instance. There is still the archaic "have no fear," but on the whole, the vocabulary much more resembles children's speech, and is much less high-flown and literary in effect.

The alphabet works well with the rhyme scheme—there is predictability about which letters come next, but not so much predictability that the story is simply a familiar alphabet song. As the Cat leaves on the last page, with the promise to return should the children ever need help cleaning up again, the words repeat the alphabet, but are arranged in a falling pattern on the page, against the backdrop of the newly whitened snow. The Cat is half off the page by the end of the story, so the reader is tempted to turn the page to see if, perhaps, there is more story to be told. Thus, Seuss uses his technique of the right-hand page as a cliff-hanger to lure the reader on. But of course, the story is over, and only the flyleaf, showing the Cat staring smugly through the window, is evident with the page turn. But the possibility of yet another sequel is clearly suggested at the end.

The story also teaches progressive diminution in size: the big Cat is clearly big, but the other cats decrease in size as their names progress through the alphabet. The book is not quite the raucous fun that the earlier book is, but the antics of the little cats as they spread the pink stain through the snow are still enjoyable to the child reader. They mimic the kinds of fun that children find in snow, except that this snow is an artificial, exotic color.

> And they jumped at the snow
> With long rakes and red bats.
> They put it in pails
> And they made high pink hills!
> Pink snow men! Pink snow balls
> And little pink pills!

The little cats spread the stain with unity and aggressiveness, with the same kind of high spirit that children exhibit in group games, much as if the task were a military target. "'Come on! Kill those spots! / Kill the mess!' yelled the cats." Their vigor and persistence in the task is obvious.

> We will clean up that snow
> If it takes us all day!
> If it takes us all night,
> We will clean it away!

Their readiness to call in reinforcements underscores their willingness to complete the task, though it also undercuts it, for with this snow, the more little cats, the more mess and the more fun.

But the story is not one about play, as was the earlier book. The opening line signals the difference. "This was no time for play." The children have been told by their mother that they must "Clean all this away." This kind of global command and faith in the children's neatness is typical of this mother, who in the earlier story believed that her children were so well behaved that they did not move from their seats for an entire rainy afternoon, did not move, never mind mess up, anything in the house.

The enormity of the children's task is underlined by the pictures: the children at the bottom of the hill, shoveling through huge drifts of snow with shovels too large for them, the house on the hill a distant goal. The children take their job seriously. Both are impatient with the Cat's interruption of their sworn duty to their mother. Though the Cat and his small cats get to play, the children do not join in, thereby showing their resolution to work, which was not clear in the earlier book. Perhaps the criticism of the Cat's behavior in the earlier book had its effect on the author. Though he could not get the Cat to behave, he could at least show that the children were right-thinking and disapproving of his behavior. Even so, the child reader participates in the pleasure of the cats' play, while at the same time experiencing the children's righteous obedience to their mother.

Fortunately for the children in the book, there is Voom to rescue the all-encompassing mess. The Voom works like a wash-day miracle, without question and immediately. It simply cleanses everything in a whirlwindlike effect; it not only straightens out the color of the snow but also manages to clear the walkways and blow all the little alphabet cats back into the big Cat's hat, presumably in alphabetical order. Its potency is apparently in inverse proportion to its size: little cat Z, like the Whos of Who-ville in *Horton Hears a Who!* is too small to be seen, yet he holds this magic ingredient under his hat. The illustration of him, on the end of the big Cat's finger, is much like that earlier illustration of the Whos, and yet his power is much more obvious—like the power of the atom bomb—unleashed when he tips his hat.

Illustration.

The visual reminiscences from the earlier story are clear. The story opens with a view of the house in inclement weather, this time snow covered, with the same bird in the same tree suffering in the same way from the precipitation. The toy boat and the cake that the Cat used in the balancing act before are now the Cat's toys in the bathtub. Also present are the same hall and the same bed—though it is now identified as Dad's bed. The cues to the first book are clearly present in the second. But though the story has more meaning when the reader is familiar with the first Cat story, still there is enough interest in the sequel that it can stand alone successfully.

The coloring of the illustration also reminds the reader of the earlier book, though the white of the page is much less obvious here, perhaps to the overall good of the story, since the persistent staining quality of the pink is the main catalyst for the whole story. The fact that the pictures are not framed on the page but extend all the way to the edge of the page, and the use of the double-page spreads, work particularly effectively here to make the enveloping of the world by pink stain efficacious and obvious. Even the text is set on a pink ground, and the pink tone is not a pastel but a particularly hot, vibrant tone, indicating the intensity of the stain and of the children's experience, especially when contrasted with the earlier pages featuring the whiteness of the snow.

Reputation.

Though *The Cat in the Hat Comes Back* has not been as big a seller as *The Cat in the Hat*, still it is one of the top ten best-sellers for children of all time.[13] Its formulaic reliance on the alphabet as a pattern for the book makes it less surprising than the earlier Cat book, which relied primarily on the surprising antics of the unpredictable Cat to delight the reader. The story indulges the child reader in messiness and vigorous play, while at the same time protecting the reader from any implication of wrongdoing. The pictures are busier, with so many more little cats cluttering up the background with their maneuvers against the snow; the growing pink tones of the page make for an even more confusing background than the white that dominates the background of the earlier Cat book. But the story is an enjoyable one, and the characters, especially the Cat, are true to their natures as established in the earlier book, and continue their intriguing manipulations of each other, much to the satisfaction of the reader. In fact, Voom is a much more satisfactory ending to the story than is the magical machine that cleans up and resolves *The Cat in the Hat,* for it is global, magical, and intense, and it involves no false pretenses of loving cleanliness as did the Cat's use of the machine. It simply disguises the fact that the children have not been able to attend to their work during the day, have been overtaken by impending disaster, and finally, as in a fairy tale, have been rescued by a supernatural agent.

I Can Read with My Eyes Shut!

The possibility of commercially successful spin-offs is difficult to resist, in spite of the frequent result that the literary quality of the subsequent works declines. In the mid-1970s, Geisel had eye trouble, which left him with black-and-white vision in one eye, and cataracts in both. Such ailments necessarily slowed down the productions of the prolific writer/illustrator, as did subsequent eye surgery. Though Geisel recovered, his inspirations were apparently temporarily at an ebb, as evidenced by the last of the books featuring the Cat as protagonist, *I Can Read with My Eyes Shut!*

The story takes the Cat and another smaller cat, addressed in the book as "Young Cat," but bearing a striking resemblance to little cat A, through a series of reading exercises—reading words printed in colors, reading words printed in circles, reading difficult words, such as "Mississippi, Indianapolis, and Hallelujah, too!"[14] Even these difficult words the big Cat claims to be able to read with his eyes shut, though he does not recommend this method. The Cat and the book's prevailing message is that reading with the eyes open is much more successful, for a number of reasons. It is faster, so that one can read about a wider variety of subjects. One is more likely not to miss something with the eyes open. One will be more learned and will be able to make more imaginative flights to different exotic places with open-eyed reading. And one is less likely to get lost, either on the imaginative flights or in the text. Overall, the book is a series of episodes all designed to recommend the pleasures of reading. It is more of a concept book than a storybook. The young cat has no lines and little personality to carry the story, except such as can be gathered from his wide-eyed amazement at the wonderful sights the Cat shows him. Even the big Cat presumes on the reader's former acquaintance with him: the only unusual thing he does is reading with his eyes shut, and even this feat, he admits, gives him trouble: "it's bad for my hat / and makes my eyebrows / get red hot."

The book is shorter than the two other Cat books, only thirty-five pages and 373 words long, compared to over sixty pages and over 1500 words each for *The Cat in the Hat* and *The Cat in the Hat Comes Back*. Clearly, Dr. Seuss abandons the limited-word list, which would not include *Mississippi, Indianapolis, Hallelujah,* or any of the made-up words, such as *Foo-Foo the Snoo,* a made-up female animal resembling a moose with high heels, a purse, and social pretentions. The book is also uncharacteristically preachy, consistently harping on the virtues and pleasures of reading, even telling children that by reading, "You might learn a way to earn a few dollars," appealing to practical, if not the most high-minded motives for reading. Though readers could gather from the experience of reading the other Cat books that reading is fun, this particular book makes its biases less-subtly known, enunciating quite clearly the viewpoints of the Beginner Book series by promoting reading so obviously.

Like Marco in *Mulberry Street,* the young cat in this book is admonished to keep his eyes open in order to catch all that the world has to interest him. The message is an ambiguous one, for it is not only reading that is more successful if one is open-eyed, it is also the world itself. The final message in the book is:

> If you read with your eyes shut
> you're likely to find

> that the place where you're going
> is far, far behind.

The picture accompanying the text shows the Cat, not reading, but driving a car through a confusing set of roads, with signs pointing to such actual places as Dallas, Schenectady, Wilkes-Barre, and Naples, but also to such mythical places as Omsk, Oz, and XYZ. Is the message of this passage that driving, like reading, with the eyes shut gets one lost? Or that it simply misguides one? The text is difficult to decipher on this point.

The colors of the illustrations are much more varied, consisting of a wide spectrum of fantasy colors in many tones. Though the range of colors might be justified in a book that extends so widely over the reading experience, the use of such a variety does not give the book the consistent image or the vibrancy of the earlier Cat books. The result is a watered-down appearance to the pages, underscored by the lack of the clear, sure black outlines that formerly illustrated the Cat. In its place are sketchy lines suggesting an outline to the Cat's body, and much use of cross-hatching, indicating shading but further muddying the sometimes complicated pictures. The Cat's subtlety of expression is gone, and only in the final picture, of the Cat and young cat looking at each other with one eye open and one eye closed, does some of the mischievous, knowing expression of the earlier Cat pictures appear. The pictures are sometimes grouped two or three to the page, sometimes on two-page spreads, echoing the varieties of reading experiences Seuss records. But such variety also confuses pacing for the beginning reader.

There is some of the earlier interest in words, recalling the earlier storybooks; *fishbones, wishbones,* and *trombones* all occur on one page, showing Seuss's ability to play with an atypical suffix, *-bones,* attached to different root words, in order to come up with words that are little like their roots. There are tongue twisters, emphasizing the changeability of meaning with the simple change of letters. The rhythm of the verse is less lilting, more choppy, because of the predominantly iambic rhythm, and the use of even shorter lines than the tetrameter used in the other Cat books. Though there are the occasional returns to the anapestic

tetrameter of the earlier books, the verse seems as uncharacteristic of the Cat as does the illustration.

The book's dedication to "David Worthen, E. G." for "Eye Guy"
and the Cat's mannerly tip of his hat on the dedication page may
give some clue to Seuss's source of inspiration. Worthen was Geisel's opthalmologist and surgeon. The book's dual message of celebrating both reading and looking at the world is no accident,
apparently inspired by the author's recent brush with sightless-
ness, and by his temporary inability to read, illustrate, or write
just before and after the surgery. As Clifton Fadiman has noted,
Seuss is a professional, rather than a confessional, writer;[15] his
personal life does not intrude into his books. *I Can Read with My
Eyes Shut* is a rarity because of the autobiographical tones coming through. The book suggests the anguish of an author who con-
templated a life of reading only by memory, and whose return to
sightedness prompted a book, if only a feeble one, celebrating
reading and sight.

The Beginner Book Philosophy

The excellence of both *The Cat in the Hat* and *The Cat in the Hat
Comes Back* stands out when compared with the rest of the Beginner Books. The ability to tell a story using less than three
hundred different words—and to extend that story to a length of
over fifteen hundred words—shows the genius of the first Beginner Book. The excellence of the books is particularly clear in the
author's creation and sustaining of character, and in his complication and resolution of plot, especially given the restricted
language.

The other Beginner Books in the Random House series, including those by Dr. Seuss, are not nearly as successful in character
or plot. In fact, some do not really tell a story but simply present
a concept, like *I Can Read with My Eyes Shut!* Some of them
present common words, usually ones that rhyme; some present
common ideas, such as household items or career choices; but
none presents a character as well realized as do the Cat books.

In general, the books are made for independent reading by a beginner reader. Their smaller format—octavo, rather than the quarto size of the Seuss storybooks—makes them more easily handled. The typeset, an easy-to-read schoolbook style, is larger than that in a Seuss storybook. While mimicking the print of the basal readers, it also helps the reader to read, with the serifs that help move the eye across the page. Seuss takes advantage of the typeset at every opportunity, enlarging it to underscore the words used for large sounds, using color for color words, having words emanate from those objects that make them, printing them upside down if that is appropriate for the text. Though such concept books are not particularly good for reading aloud, they are geared for the shorter attention and perseverance of the beginning reader. Dropping a book in the middle does not interrupt the flow of a succession of two-page spreads that are not necessarily consecutive. Most Beginner Books have fewer words per page, and fewer words overall, than *The Cat in the Hat* has, thus simplifying a simple form even more.

The later books depend more intently on the illustrations to tell the story than did the earlier ones, and the illustrations depend more and more on the reader's familiarity with earlier Seuss books and characters. The variety of colors used, sometimes changing with each page, and usually not limited to two colors, makes the books more colorful but, at the same time, less unified than *The Cat in the Hat* and its sequel. Because there are sometimes two pictures per page, the backgrounds are less well developed and the pictures are smaller, sometimes confusing a beginning reader who may not adjust his visual scanning from a two-page spread to two pictures per page. The young reader might thus misinterpret four pictures on a two-page spread as somehow one picture. The books do succeed according to the standards set for them, as announced in their promotional material on the covers and on the end pages—"exacting blends of words and pictures that encourage children to read—all by themselves."[16] But the storybooks remain better sources of stories and more successful books in general.

In fact, the Beginner Books border on printing rather than on literature. They are more "readers" than storybooks. They do teach certain aspects about books that new readers need to learn. The Beginner Books demonstrate the correspondence between pictures and text. They show that the print usually is not part of the picture but is a caption that describes what is going on in the picture. The words and story progress from left to right, and from front to back. Pages are turned one at a time. Persons on one page are not different from the same people illustrated on the next page. Books in English are read with the spine on the left when opening the book. Covers to books include the title of the book and sometimes a picture of someone in the book, but the cover does not begin the body of the story. Finally, the Beginner Books show that spoken language is different from the language found in books. Adults and older children understand all of these conventions about books, but beginning readers, especially those who have no experience with books as objects other than toys, do not understand and must learn. But the books in the series that succeeded *The Cat in the Hat Comes Back* are not short stories but are more like short narrative vignettes. Usually the rhyme aspires not to poetry, but remains simply short verse or even just a list of words that happen to rhyme. There is sometimes little attempt at sustained narrative. For adults and older child readers, the Beginner Books will have little enduring interest, though the books do succeed with younger readers, their intended audience.

But perhaps that is the design of the series—first, to give children an introduction to the culture of the book, to acquaint them with the power and significance of the printed word and their ability to master at least the simplest of them; and then to move them on to books that are more technically literature. Though older children return to some of the Beginner Books even when they are competent readers, it is usually a return to personal favorites, and not an indication of a preference for the simpler books. Frequently, older children may consider these earlier books too babyish, too simple, and too silly for their more advanced ages. But the books do "encourage children to read—all by themselves," and once the competence to do so is developed, children can safely move on.

Language.

Nearly all the Dr. Seuss Beginner Books are in verse, gratifying children by providing predictability to the narration—an unknown word must have a sound that conforms to the accentual pattern of the line, and must sound something like the rhyme word that precedes it. The use of rhyme may also gratify the adult who provides the book for the child, since it quickly develops additional vocabulary words, and also demands precision in the reading—words that look similar are not alike, and may have completely different meanings. Though *The Cat in the Hat* is a masterpiece in using only words on a prescribed list of vocabulary for first-grade readers, the later books take considerably more liberty with language. The prescribed vocabulary list is abandoned, in favor of words that early elementary-school children will certainly have in their speaking vocabulary, but that are sometimes multisyllabic, with sound patterns that are atypical of the usual rules of phonics.

The books do have interesting covers, one sure way to lure a child to pick up a book, and colorful inside pictures. The Cat in the Hat logo for the Beginner Book series, with the caption "I Can Read It All by Myself," reassures the child reader, who may recognize the Cat and his contented, smug look, and therefore assume that this book is similar to the other Cat books. It also reassures the buyer, most likely an adult, that this is an appropriate book for the young reader, and a reliable product, issued by the same publishing house that produced *The Cat in the Hat.* A quick turn to the end pages or back cover yields a description of the philosophy behind the Beginner Book series, which reassures adult purchasers that these are indeed educational books appropriate for young readers, and that these books, though educational, are supposed to be fun.

The connection between picture and text is strong. The beginning reader will not be confused by details and will be able to "read" the picture if for some reason the language is not immediately accessible. Though there may not be enough interest to sustain frequent rereading by an adult, there is enough for the child, whose sense of mastery over both picture and word, and whose willingness to tolerate repetition of both, simply aid the learning process.

The language for the most part is that of the child's world— simple household items, concepts, body parts, activities. These words, frequently atypical of basal readers, are ones which a five- or six-year-old will understand, and will have as part of his working spoken vocabulary. The books simply bridge the gap between a child's sight vocabulary, those words that a child can actually read, and his total vocabulary, those that he recognizes, even if he does not commonly use them. As his output for the series progressed, Dr. Seuss came to rely more and more on the predictability and redundancy of language, and the context of both picture and language to define difficult words. He came to trust the child reader's linguistic competence and his willingness to learn reading if the process were made pleasurable and challenging, if not too difficult. Though most of the words are actual words, there are those books that depend on made-up words, a sort of pseudovocabulary. *There's a Wocket in My Pocket!* defines typical words by rhyming them with made-up ones, as in the title. The effect is humorous, but one which will appeal to children, and will make the reading process fun.

In fact, all the books are fun. There is not a serious volume among them. A steady diet of these Beginner Books probably would not satisfy either a child or an adult, but they are enjoyable and will begin a child's reading career with both pleasure and mastery. The more serious issues of life, such as those that Dr. Seuss investigates in the larger, longer storybooks, are not appropriate fare for introducing the child to reading. Such issues are more properly introduced in spoken words, or held in abeyance until the child is more competent in reading. The Beginner Books work on the "simple premise that children will believe a ludicrous situation if pursued with relentless logic."[17] The incongruity that results appeals to children if not to adults, but this series avoids the pitfall of many beginning books. Not a single title in the Beginner Book series is cute, so cute that the child reader will feel patronized, or the adult reader offended.

The task of paring down vocabulary to an even more limited

list than that used in *The Cat in the Hat* attracted Dr. Seuss as an intellectual challenge, one that resulted in such Beginner Books as *Hop on Pop* (1963) and *Ten Apples up on Top!* (1961), a book published under Seuss's other pseudonym, Theo. LeSieg. *Hop on Pop* even includes the promise on the cover that it is "the Simplest Seuss for Youngest Use." Seuss was inspired to write the first of these severely limited books, *Green Eggs and Ham,* by a dare from Bennett Cerf, his editor, that Seuss write a book of fifty words or less.[18] The emphasis in both books on the acquisition of simple rhyming vocabulary is evident not only in the short sentences, usually five or fewer words long, but also in the repetition of the rhyme words in large print on each page, and in the dictionary-illustration of the rhyme words in lists on the end pages. Underneath the Beginner Books logo on the cover, *Ten Apples* displays the sign 75 Word Vocabulary, and though the illustration by Roy McKie may not permit a child reader to immediately recognize the book as a Dr. Seuss product, the intent to educate by pleasing is still clear to the adult buyer. The book is also a counting game, helping the child to learn the written words corresponding to numbers. The educational value of the book is underscored by the counting, which also provides tension—will the animals on the cover be able to balance ten apples on their heads?

The philosophy behind the Beginner Books, though not necessarily scientific or based on extensive research into the teaching and learning of reading, is rooted in common sense, and has been proven effective by past successes. The philosophy advocates a tightly executed plot with close correspondence between text and illustration; a simplified, if no longer a limited, vocabulary; short sentences, preferably in rhyme; nothing in the text that is not pictured in the illustrations; no more than one illustration per page; and no vocabulary that a child will not be able to read, even though he might recognize the word in speech. Overall, the Beginner Books seek to bridge the "gap between the breadth of interest of most six-year-olds and the limitations of the reading matter available to them."[19] As Seuss himself has said, this list of requirements means that all the lovely adjectives and long descriptions must go.[20] The requirements, though simple, have meant for Seuss much revision of his text, and much longer periods of composition than most readers would expect, given the brevity of the books—up to a year, in some cases; more typically, nine or ten months.

Bright and Early Books.

This impulse to produce books using a more limited vocabulary and a tighter relationship between picture and text resulted in the Bright and Early series of books, which Seuss described as "an attempt to initiate very young children into the mysteries of reading by seeing to it that almost every word in the text is neatly juxtaposed with an illustration of the object it describes."[21] In an interview, Dr. Seuss admits that Bright and Early books are a modification of the Beginner Books, with half the number of pages, and a tighter interaction between picture and words. The vocabulary in the Bright and Early series "will send a child to first grade with a knowledge of most of the words he'll learn in first grade,"[22] and with a sense of books as books and not as mere toys.

This severe proscription on text and illustration leads to even less interest for an adult reader, but more for a child reader. The books are modifications of books for babies, which include only one picture and one word on a page. Such books are frequently made of cloth or cardboard, so that they will survive a small child's handling and mishandling of them. But the Bright and Early books are clearly books, with hard covers and paper pages like the Beginner Books, though with even less narrative. The emphasis in the books is on simple concepts—feet, eyes, animal sounds, shapes—in fact, just the kind of words that children will know and will learn to read early in their reading careers. The books frequently invite the child reader to participate, as is clear from the title of *Mr. Brown Can Moo! Can You?* which invites the child to mimic Mr. Brown's sounds. Though there are some made-up words, the language is mostly realistic, and the fun is mostly in the pictures.

In several interviews, Dr. Seuss has jokingly admitted to contemplating a series of prenatal books, though how these books would deliver their messages to the intended audience has baffled him. The Bright and Early books do introduce children only slightly older than infants to reading and to books. But they do so in a particularly American way, with a clear concern for getting children to read as early as possible, and getting them to first grade having already mastered all that they will learn in first grade. Since Puritan times, Americans have emphasized the importance of reading, though there has been some variation throughout history in opinions about how early children should learn. But as Bruno Bettelheim has pointed out in his book titled *On Reading,* the United States has one of the highest failure rates in literacy in the developed world. Bettelheim attributes this failure partly to the kind of material children learn to read with—basal readers that insult their intelligence and provide little interest,[23] the quality of which John Hersey questioned in 1954 in the *Life* magazine article where he called on Dr. Seuss to produce an alternative.

But part of the reason for this rate of failure may also be attributed to the pressure Americans place on learning to read. The Bright and Early books respond to this pressure, but they do not provide the "ideal introduction to the world of books" that their publishers claim for them on the books' end pages. They do introduce children to reading on their own, but they do not provide interesting stories, nor do they encourage adults to read the books aloud to children more than once or twice. In other words, children fed a steady diet of these books will most likely see adults who are bored with the books, rather than the more positive example of adults who are enjoying them. The Bright and Early and Beginner Books series are introductions to reading, it is true, but children need much more variety and complexity in their reading to sustain interest in the process. The books are an alternative to basal readers, but they stand in their stead; they are not the kind of "real" literature alternatives to the basal reader that Bettelheim suggests children need to practice their reading.

Marketing.

The success of both series of books has rested on the marketing of them; *The Cat in the Hat* was first issued both as a textbook and as a trade book, thereby appealing to both markets. Library bindings for the books are available, making them attractive purchases both for school and public libraries. But the less expensive trade bindings and the reasonable prices on the books have not made them the upscale choice of purchase by those who want an elegant children's book. Instead, the books are available in toy stores, department stores, even discount stores and pharmacies. Though more expensive than the Golden Books series, which is sold primarily in grocery stores, they are also more durable, yet not so highly priced that their loss or damage would mean a significant cost to replace them. The use of the Cat in the Hat in the logo makes the books marketable simply by the recognition granted to the Cat.

Many of the reissues of the books contain the same advertising on the back cover or inside on the end pages, a quotation from Ellen Goodman about the initial success of *The Cat in the Hat.* The first issues featured advertisements particularly tailored to the individual book. For example, *Wacky Wednesday,* a book that requires the reader to look for mistakes in the pictures, has the Beginner Books logo upside down on the cover. And though Ellen Goodman's words still appear on the back cover, inside the front cover is a brief description of *Wacky Wednesday,* with the promise that as the young readers "hunt for all the wonderfully silly things that are wrong on each page, they'll also discover that they are reading—all by themselves."[24] The Bright and Early books feature a quotation on the back from Margaret B. Parke, professor at Brooklyn College, with the publicity blurb that "the Cat in the Hat proudly presents books for the youngest of the young!" with the educational benefits that "the stories are brief and funny, the words are few and easy and have a happy, catching rhythm, and the pictures are clear and colorful clues to the text." It seems that though Americans want their children to read, they do not want them to have fun without acquiring some piece of knowledge as well. The words of approval by an educational expert, even if it is one unknown to the adult, help reassure the adult that children should be allowed to have fun.

As John Gough notes, a further reassurance to the adult buyer is the stories' featuring of middle-class settings and values. Even in those stories that venture out of the United States, such as *Come Over to My House,* which features a tour of houses all over the world, no extremely rich or extremely poor children are pictured; everyone, all over the world, has a house, one that he can be proud to invite another child from another country to play in. The jobs in *Maybe You Should Fly a Jet! Maybe You Should be a Vet!* are all dignified and interesting, thus glorifying the Protestant work ethic while ignoring issues of unemployment and underemployment.[25] No American parent would object to anything in these books, thus assuring their salesworthiness.

Pseudonyms.

In the Beginner Book series are books by Dr. Seuss written under two other pseudonyms—Theo. LeSieg and Rosetta Stone. These books are not illustrated by Dr. Seuss, but by several other illustrators, the most prominent of whom is Roy McKie. The LeSieg books appear with the Beginner Book logo, and a separate list of Beginner Books by Theo. LeSieg at the end, with cryptic statements about the author having "as his mentor, Dr. Seuss" *(Maybe You Should Be a Vet),* or the fact that "Theo. LeSieg and Dr. Seuss have led almost mystically parallel lives." Lingeman reports that Seuss considers the LeSieg pseudonym for "books that won't make a good Seuss," and then provides the text with specific suggestions for another illustrator.[26] On inquiry from Gough, Geisel admitted that he resorts to the pseudonyms to fill out his list of new books each publishing season. The LeSieg books need other illustrators because, as Geisel says, "most of them call for more realistic animals than he [Seuss] likes to do, or for human characters that he doesn't do very well at all."[27] The Stone pseudonym is clearly a joke about the Rosetta Stone, which permitted archaeologists to interpret Sanskrit, but its use is the same as the LeSieg name—for books that the author chooses not to illustrate himself.

Though the change of illustrators certainly makes a difference in the experience of the book, these books follow the same patterns as the other Beginner Books. Seuss's desire to have another illustrator sometimes seems less dictated by the content of the book than by personal preference. The variety of illustrators certainly makes the Beginner and Bright and Early series more varied, but that seems to be the only virtue of varying illustrators. Seuss himself has admitted that the combination of writer and illustrator in one person makes for more successful books, at least artistically and literarily if not commercially.[28] But overall, the use of the two other pseudonyms seems just another device to market more Dr. Seuss books.

Green Eggs and Ham

Of all the Dr. Seuss books, *Green Eggs and Ham* has been the best seller. In fact, it tops the list of "Children's Book Best Sellers, 1895–1975" compiled in *80 Years of Best Sellers, 1895–1975* (1977 Xerox),[29] leading four other Beginner Books by Dr. Seuss in the top eight, including *The Cat in the Hat* and its sequel. Because of its popularity, the book is singled out here for special comment. The book is repetitive and short—671 words long, containing 51 different words—and resembles a Bright and Early book in its word length and repetition.

The story of Sam and his unnamed but larger companion is easily told: Sam suggests to his friend that he eat green eggs and green ham, but the friend replies that he does not like them. Sam suggests he sample the food in a number of different places and with a number of different companions, but the friend is adamant until Sam wears him down, pestering him with the food. When the friend relents, he finds that he does like the food, and thanks Sam.

What is missing in the summary of the story is the intensity of Sam's questions and the repetition in the answers of the terms of the questions. The pattern of the book is based on cumulative verse, giving the book its form: Sam suggests, the friend answers, summarizing all the various suggestions that have come before. Sam's suggestions are really irrelevant to the appeal of the food; eating green eggs and green ham "in a house" or "with a mouse"[30] makes no difference to their taste. But the friend, who as an adult should know better, is as relentless in his refusal to taste as Sam is in his suggestions.

The story is humorous, which is one of its virtues, and highly repetitive, using the same vocabulary, so that once it is mastered, the child can continue to use it in the rest of the book. The amount of text on each page lengthens as the possibilities that Sam suggests are recalled, thus encouraging the child to remember the story as it goes on, and to use that memory to help him remember the words. The story also builds up slowly, from the three words on the first page, "I am Sam," to the twelve lines, near the end of the book, recalling all of Sam's suggestions, which result in the friend's acquiescence—"If you will let me be,"—to Sam's request that he try the food. These twelve lines are accompanied by a picture that includes reminiscences of those suggestions, thus helping the child reader's recall of the new vocabulary.

The resolution is a quick one; the friend's mind is changed when he simply does what Sam asks, and the chaos that has resulted from Sam's dragging his friend through all his suggestions—on a train, on a goat, on a boat—is quickly resolved on the final page, with a picture of the empty platter that before held the green eggs and ham, the friend's arm around Sam, and a twice-repeated "Thank you!" In usual Seuss fashion, the tension builds as the number of objects in the book increases, and then is quickly and easily resolved into a happy ending. Purves and Monson have claimed that the argument over food is one of the book's appeals.[31] Such arguments are clearly part of a child's life and dealings with parents, who try to coax foods, especially green ones such as vegetables, down children's throats with absurd promises that they will taste good. The bright green of the food here—like the artificial green of Oobleck—does not predispose the food to look appetizing, and the child may find himself sympathizing with the friend who tries to decline Sam's offer. Like a waiter, Sam holds the platter on one open hand, as if advertising its specialness. But even the cover casts doubt on the food's real quality, as the friend looks askance at the platter. In his avidity, Sam resembles someone who is trying too hard to sell his product. But some salesmen, like some parents, and even some children, really do know their products; the swift ending is the only possible one to an argument about food, and both child and adult reader will recognize that.

Although the child reader may sympathize with the friend, Sam has his appeal as well. Sam is a pest, as Monson and Purves have rightly called him.[32] Children must deal with being pestered and nagged in their lives, but they can also be pests themselves. Because this pest is a small person who knows what he is talking about, the child may identify with Sam as well as with the friend. While the friend's consistent sourness through the story makes him unattractive, the certainty with which he answers "I do not like green eggs and ham" rings as true to children as Sam's claim that "You may like them." That there are two characters for a child reader to recognize as like himself only doubles the book's potential for success.

Monson and Purves have also pointed to the book's cartoonlike drawings as part of its success.[33] Sam and his friend are doglike, Grinchlike, and human at the same time. They are clearly characters of fantasy, with preposterous high hats that slouch like the Cat in the Hat's. The pictures all move from left to right, some with startling speed, such as the ones with Sam and friend on the train. There is even one two-page spread without any text, when the friend, still unsure, takes the platter in one hand and a fork in the other, with a still-doubtful look, as Sam and all the other characters in the book look on expectantly and the tension builds before the resolution. Certainly the recognizable Dr. Seuss style has promoted the book's popularity, but the fact remains that this is the best-seller of all the Dr. Seuss best-sellers. The combination of recognizable author/illustrator; two characters who both appeal to the child reader; the nature of the argument; and the middle-ground vocabulary, with fewer words than the earlier Beginner Books but longer length than the Bright and Early books, have all guaranteed this book's success and longevity.

5

The Later "Message" Books

After a period of mediocre books, both the longer storybooks and the shorter Beginner and Bright and Early Books, Dr. Seuss made the headlines again with a frank, devastating allegory about ecology, *The Lorax.* During the period between *The Cat in the Hat* and *The Lorax,* the author's phenomenal output continued. But the Beginner Books represent a beginning of an end. John P. Bailey, Jr., writing in 1965, viewed the Beginner Books as "the beginning of a rather crass marketing approach to Dr. Seuss's output. The engaging fun of the previous periods is lost in a marked forcing of ideas." Bailey further designated *Happy Birthday to You!* as "the zenith (or is it nadir?) of this period," a title that succeeded because it was written as the perfect birthday gift for children, and was bound to sell, in spite of its unsure handling of color and forced rhymes. Bailey also singled out *The Dr. Seuss Sleep Book* as another book written for "solely commercial aims," and claimed that in the Beginner Books, Dr. Seuss "has lost the intimacy and friendliness which endeared him to both children and parents."[1] Even the storybooks of the period trudge along in forced order, with uninspired pictures and even less inviting plots and characters.

But while he was tending to the Beginner Books and Bright and Early series, he was simply biding his time. In the last two decades, the most remarkable of Dr. Seuss's books have been the "message" books about issues that adults generally consider adult concerns. Because of his depth of feeling about the issues of ecology and nuclear disarmament, Seuss risked negative publicity in publishing these books. But perhaps because of his long-standing following, established through his work on the Beginner Books, the risk paid off; all three of the later books examined in this chapter reached the best-seller list.

The Lorax

In 1971, Dr. Seuss broke away from the business of producing storybooks and managing the Beginner Books division of Random House to write a passionate allegory about pollution—its causes and the solutions. *The Lorax* is Dr. Seuss's personal favorite,[2] though he admits it has not been one of his best-selling titles. The book was made into a television special for the CBS network, which necessitated some toning down of the criticism of big business in the book, in order not to offend the program's commercial sponsors. But of all the Seuss books, *The Lorax* is the most strident and most thinly veiled of all the allegories, and its message, both to big businesses and young readers, is crystal clear.

The Lorax is a small, wizened old creature who represents the wildlife in the story. The villain of the piece is the Once-ler, who now lives in a dreary, nearly deserted town and for a price tells his story to a curious boy. The Once-ler was once a pioneer with a Conestoga wagon, who happened upon an untouched natural paradise, in which he decided to settle. The Once-ler finds that the tufts of the native Truffula trees make excellent yarn for knitting a Thneed, a shapeless, useless garment that becomes faddishly popular and sells well. As the Once-ler cuts down the first tree, the Lorax appears to protest the interference with the natural environment, though the Once-ler assures him that one less tree does no harm.

But the lure of money induces all the Once-lers to settle and knit Thneeds, and the resulting factory pollutes both air and water. The Lorax protests on behalf of the Bar-ba-loots, the fish, and the swans, all of whom leave the area, but the Once-ler will not listen to the Lorax's dire predictions. Finally, when the last tree is cut and the whole landscape is ruined, the Lorax disappears into the air, leaving behind a monument like a tomb, with a stone marker cryptically inscribed "Unless."[3] The Once-ler explains to the boy who is listening to the story that

> UNLESS someone like you
> cares a whole awful lot,
> nothing is going to get better.
> It's not.

With these parting words, the Once-ler entrusts to the boy the last existing Truffula seed, and bids him plant and tend it.

The character of the Lorax derives from the tradition of the small, wise creature, humanlike, but not quite, and clearly child sized. Even the Once-ler admits that the Lorax is hard to describe, though "It was sort of a man." His appearance on the stump of the first Truffula tree that is axed suggests that he is a nature spirit, living in the tree and liberated by the chopping. It also suggests that he needs a soapbox or a pulpit to deliver his message, which he does in a particularly annoying tone. "And he spoke with a voice / that was sharpish and bossy." He is clearly some kind of messenger or supernatural guardian of living but defenseless things, for as he says, "I speak for the trees, for the trees have no tongues." He also asserts possession over these things, calling them "my Truffula tuft," and "My poor Swomeee-Swans," though the possessive pronoun seems inappropriate for a spirit of nature whose message asserts the responsibility of all creatures for the welfare of others, especially those unable to defend themselves. His beard and his age, which both his picture and the Once-ler acknowledge, give him the right to be peremptory and nearly rude.

The Once-ler's actions certainly require this assertive tone, though it initiates an uncharacteristic name-calling between the two characters that suggests the vehemence of the author's feelings about the issues in the book. The Lorax says that the Once-

ler is "crazy with greed," and that "There is no one on earth / who
would buy that fool Thneed," implying that the Thneed-maker is
a fool as well. But when the Thneed sells, the Once-ler counters
with "You poor stupid guy!" Later, the Lorax returns with "You
dirty old Once-ler man, you," an ambiguous insult about the
Once-ler's tainting of the environment, and perhaps about his
sexual proclivities too. But the shouting match ends with the
Once-ler calling the Lorax "Dad," an insult that denigrates both
his age and his wisdom and is overly familiar. The "shut up, if
you please" in midstory, with its shift in levels of diction, is evidence of the way the two characters conduct their argument.
They are rude at the same time they invoke higher, loftier language and goals.

But the Once-ler's goals, though they sound like old adages and
common sense, are not nearly so lofty. "Business is business! /
And business must grow" is a typical American attitude, adopted
when the resources of the continent seemed limitless, and when
a growth economy was the only way known to measure business
success and prosperity. Though concepts of a stable-state economy, where growth is not an issue and where resources are scarce
and expensive, have gradually evolved, most Americans would
agree that bigger is better and what is good for business is good
for America. As an opponent, the Lorax offers yet another American attitude, of plain talking without sugarcoating or pleading,
and of vigilant defense of the defenseless. When the boy describes
the spot where the Lorax leaves his pile of stones, he talks of the
place where "you can still see, today, / where the Lorax once stood
/ just as long as it could," a monument that has mythic overtones,
like the Alamo and its defenders.

The Lorax points out the problems involved in the conduct of
business, especially manufacturing industries—destruction of
some natural resources with no concern for replacing them, and
pollution of the rest of the natural habitat, with the destruction
of animals. Mercifully, the animals here do not die, though they
do suffer: the Bar-ba-loots have "crummies in [their] tummies,"
the Swomee-Swans have smog in their throats, and the Humming
Fish have gunk in their gills. But the Lorax is a good guardian,

sending them off before they die, though it is not clear where they will go. The Lorax's odd but grammatically correct use of *hopefully* in "I don't hopefully know" underscores that there is some hope for them, but the specifics of the hope are unclear.

In his tale of the Thneed as the Once-ler's manufactured item, Dr. Seuss spreads the blame for the destruction wrought to make it. If there were no market for the Thneed, the manufacture of it would not have satisfied the Once-ler's desire for money, which he claims that "everyone needs," an adage that goes unquestioned in the action of the book but not necessarily in the mature reader's mind. But because the Lorax is wrong when he says, "There is no one on earth / who would buy that fool Thneed!" the buying public becomes a fool, and the Once-ler is seen to possess the wisdom of a P. T. Barnum when he says, "You never can tell what some people will buy." And because the public is convinced that the Thneed, a misshapen garment like a pajama with odd sleeves and legs, is "a Fine-Something-That-All-People-Need," the destruction of the Truffula trees begins, and there is no outcry, no boycott, no public questioning of the disastrous events that ensue.

In the name of bigger business and profits and "biggering" his business, the Once-ler begins building. His first act of destruction comes in the simple unloading of his covered wagon, when he randomly throws things out onto the green grass, tools and supplies that contrast sharply with the Edenic paradise he has found. He starts by building, first a small shop; then a radio phone by which he calls his relatives to come to his factory, which he then builds; and then a "Super-Axe-Hacker," which only hastens the destruction of the Truffula forest. It is noteworthy that the only feature of the Once-ler that appears in the book, with the exception of the eyes that peer out at the boy in the beginning of the story, are his hands, human ones with four fingers and a thumb. The lack of a physical body for the Once-ler allows the reader to imagine the worst, to horrify himself even more than Dr. Seuss can do. But the hands are significant, for they are always busy, always manipulating, never caressing or cherishing, never simply lying idle. Though industry and work with the hands are highly admired by Americans, here the results of such handiness are apparent—a disregard for everything they touch, with the possible exception of money. That the Once-ler places the last Truffula seed into the hands of the boy is important, for the Once-ler's hands have wrought only destruction. Someone with untainted hands must take over the job of restoration.

But this job will not be an easy one. The Once-ler's name, implying that he uses things only once, or that things will stand his using them only once, also suggests that once upon a time things were better. But getting back the Lorax and his friends will be more than just a matter of reforesting with Truffula trees and protecting the trees from lumbering interests. The Once-ler tells the boy that he must care for the seed and "give it clean water. And feed it fresh air," tasks that will not be easy given the desolation of the landscape. And even should he succeed in reforesting, the Once-ler offers the boy only the hope that "the Lorax / and all of his friends / may come back." There is no certainty, though there is hope. The blank two-page spread at the end of the book almost invites the reader to fill it in with a vision of what the restored landscape will look like.

The degree of the destruction is particularly devastating when compared with the landscape at the point of the Once-ler's arrival. He himself calls it "this glorious place" and evokes images of paradise when he starts his story with "Way back in the days when the grass was still green / and the pond was still wet / and the clouds were still clean." The contrast to the darkened, deserted town, where only "Grickle-grass grows," and the air smells, and even the lamppost has difficulty standing upright, is especially dramatic, since only darker shades of blue, green, and violet lend color to the destroyed landscape, while bright yellows, pinks, and shades of green that approach the natural adorn the untouched landscape. The Humming-Fish, the Bar-ba-loots, and the Swomee-Swans are all familiar-looking creatures from earlier Seuss books, but they cavort here with childlike innocence and abandon, having nothing to do but play, hum, sing, and eat all day in a lush, warm landscape. All the viewer's senses are appealed to in the description of this Eden, with the songs of the swans and hums of the fish, and the taste and the sight of the

Truffula fruits. The qualities of the Truffula foliage, the most obvious aspect of the landscape that the Once-ler describes, appeal to both touch and smell. "The touch of their tufts was much softer than silk / And they had the sweet smell of fresh butterfly milk." The dank, cold landscape will have to be nearly resurrected to achieve this kind of appeal again.

But that is the boy's job, and there is never any question that he might not succeed. It is the only hope offered in the book, but a particularly salient one for the young reader, since it is a child who will save this world. The boy is a passive listener throughout the story, and appears only at the beginning and at the end. But his charge to care for the Truffula seed arouses him to action, just as Dr. Seuss undoubtedly hoped that child readers would be roused to action on behalf of the environment. Planting seeds is a small gesture, one that children can accomplish, and may be a simplification of the efforts that must take place to restore a damaged environment. But simply raising awareness of pollution, and giving children some specific action to take against it, is probably all that an author can suggest without turning a children's book into a blatant piece of propaganda for a particular political issue.

The Lorax is a model for the child reader of yet another course of action—the reader can speak out and oppose the actions of polluters with strong environmental advocacy. The frankness, even the rudeness, of the Lorax indicates the stridency that Dr. Seuss permits the reader to use in opposing polluters; the extent of the destruction in the book, where there is only hope, but no assurance, of reclamation of the landscape at the end, justifies this assertive stance, even in children. Showing the stupidity of consumers, as they thoughtlessly purchase useless objects whose production entails pollution, offers another course of action, albeit a more indirect one: even a child can refuse to consume products that are useless. The question of what should be done about necessary commodities whose manufacture also pollutes or destroys—antibiotics, heat, products for home building—is not answered here, but as a simple call to action, the book is a success.

The initial reviewers of the book were divided about the book's

ability to rouse the reader, and about the appropriateness of in-
citing children to action over ecology. That the book was not as
commercially successful as other Seuss titles may indicate that
the obvious moralizing here was not popular with the children's
book–buying public, since this is not a simple, amusing book that
aims primarily to teach children to read. It is also a clear exception to Dr. Seuss's occasional claim that he is not a particularly
strong moralist in his books, a claim that may hold elsewhere but
not in *The Lorax*. The television version was a great success, and
combined with the book's colorful cover and pictures (at least before the Once-ler gets going with the Thneeds), has guaranteed
the book's continuation in print.

The Butter Battle Book

Of all Dr. Seuss's books, *The Butter Battle Book* is the most controversial because it deals with mutually assured self-destruction
by nuclear weapons. Though young children may not see the parallel between the arms race and the story in the book, older children and adults definitely will. Some reviewers have expressed
their surprise, even their dismay, on picking up the book and
reading it to children without previewing it first, only to find that
the Dr. Seuss name on the cover did not guarantee the simple,
fun book that they had expected. Some critics have questioned
introducing young children to such weighty world problems, their
assumption being that this book is intended for the same youthful
audience as the Dr. Seuss Beginner Books. But the subject matter
defies categorization by ages or even by stages of development. In
the final analysis, the book is as much for adults as it is for children, and judicious use of it with children can lead to some startling but heartening responses from them.

The Butter Battle is a war fought between the Yooks and Zooks,
human-looking animals with bald heads and beaks for mouths.
The issue in the war is whether it is right to butter one's bread
right side up, as the Yooks believe, or upside down, as the Zooks
believe. The story is told by a grandfather Yook, a military officer

designated to start the war. The conflict in beliefs is one of long-standing, having started with a simple low wall between the two territories, but then escalating into a higher wall with border patrols, who respond to each other's increasingly sophisticated armaments with both defensive and offensive weapons of ever-increasing size and sophistication. There are no shots fired, no weapons actually used, the scare tactics of both sides being as effective as their weapons. But as the story progresses, the Yooks, who live in peaceful coexistence with the Zooks, albeit on opposite sides of a wall, become increasingly militant, with brass bands and cheerleaders egging on their military heroes. The issue of buttering bread becomes one of national pride and honor, to be fought over to the death. The ultimate weapon for both sides is the Bitsy Big-Boy Boomeroo, a small pellet with the capacity to blow up all the Zooks, while the Yooks wait in an underground bunker for the war to be won for them.

The book's ending is unresolved, for the Zooks also have a Boomeroo, and their war hero faces the Yooks' war hero, both threatening to drop the ultimate weapon. The final page shows the two of them facing each other with Boomeroos poised for dropping, and the small Yook grandchild looking on, anxiously asking his grandfather, the war hero: "Who's going to drop it? / Will *you* . . . ? Or will *he*. . . ?" The grandfather answers, "Be patient. . . . We'll see. / We will see. . . ."[4] The final ellipsis ending the book is Dr. Seuss's usual device for indicating a cliff-hanger that urges the reader on to the next page, assisting the forward, rightward movement of the book and the pictures. But this is the end of the book, and the final page is on the left, facing a blank right page. Does the blank page indicate total destruction? Or does it, as in *The Lorax*, indicate that the reader should fill in his own vision of the end?

In numerous interviews about the book, Dr. Seuss has claimed that posing any ending would make the book propagandistic and unrealistic as well, since the answer in real life is not at all clear. By using this open ending, Dr. Seuss violates one of the prime conventions of children's literature—that works for children should have closed endings, preferably happy ones, with all important questions answered and with no loose ends left unresolved. But for Seuss's purposes, there can be no resolution. He places the burden of finishing the story squarely in the lap of the reader.

The endings that children pose frequently depend on their ages. In an interview in *USA Today* shortly after the publication of *The Butter Battle Book,* Seuss reported receiving many letters from children with their versions of the endings. Though some children "hope the Yooks knock the badinage out of the Zooks," the more "average answer" seems to have been, "Why don't we sit down and talk it over?"[5] The child respondents here are clearly old enough to read and write, since they sent their letters to Dr. Seuss. But Nancy Carlsson-Paige and Diane E. Levin have reported that preschoolers have different reactions to the story. Though more sophisticated readers will perceive that the issue of which side to butter one's bread is ridiculous and trivial, younger children take the matter seriously, as if the question clearly needs answering, and think that the Zooks, since they are the ones who defy common sense, need converting. Carlsson-Paige and Levin have advised that such young children need concrete solutions, arrived at by such tactics as having the children play the parts of Yooks or Zooks. When the Yooks assert, with the narcissism typical of young children, that they are right, the children playing Zooks can explain their points of view, thus emphasizing that there can be a variety of different points of view, and that all can be right, or at least value-neutral, at the same time.[6]

Carlsson-Paige and Levin also point to certain abuses of the book by adults, such as dwelling on the fact that there are such powerful bombs in real life as the Boomeroo, poised for use, and that all human life is terribly tenuous with such a threat hanging over it. For children who cannot even contemplate their own deaths, and for whom the death of a parent is the worst possible event, such a threat leads either to a healthy denial of the threat and the childlike assurance that everything is really fine, thus avoiding the book's message about the need for tolerance and negotiation, or to severe emotional consequences. Ideally, the book should elicit discussion and action, not paralyzing terror or denial.[7]

The book also has a message for adults. Daniel R. Bechtel, reviewer for the *Christian Century,* reported the experience of reading the story aloud to his grandson without previewing it. The book was clearly a surprise, not only to grandson and grandfather, but also to the child's parents. After reading part of it, the whole family immediately turned to a nature book, as if to reassert that the terrifying issues would go away, and that everything, like the birds in the book, was fine and beautiful. The family did not reread the book, but Bechtel began to think about the grandfather in the book telling the story to his grandson, and about his own role as a grandfather, retelling the story to his own grandson. The human grandfather was clearly moved to action by a feeling that he needed to protect the world for his grandson and not let the ultimate destruction occur; to do so would be to take the role of the warmonger Yook grandfather. Bechtel pointed out that the blank page at the end of the book is a useful literary device, not simply a fluke of book design. Clearly one of Seuss's more thoughtful readers and reviewers, Bechtel noted that the implication of the book for adults is that they must protect children and keep the world safe for them.[8]

Seuss's portrayal of the Yooks and the Zooks as similar disturbed some reviewers. In his *Commonweal* review of the book, John Garvey pointed out that arms proliferation is not a result of trivial differences of opinions. Garvey claimed that the book does not admit that there are actual evils in the world, but simply that there are differences of opinion over essentially meaningless issues.[9] The *National Review* also pointed to the trivialization of the arms race in the book, and the book's perhaps inadvertent message that arms proliferation has resulted in deterrence. No one in the book is harmed, no weapon is actually used. This review also pointed out that the word *Yooks* sounds like *Yanks,* and that the Zooks must clearly be the Russians, since they wear red suits, in contrast to the Yooks' blue ones.[10] The obviously political nature of the book invites these interpretations, but the author's point is that there is little difference between the two sides in the arms race; though the original inspiration was to create two entirely different cultures for the Yooks and the Zooks, "what I was trying to say was that the Yooks and the Zooks were intrinsically

the same. The more I made them different, the more I was de-
feating the story."[11] The appeal to a child's perception is clear here.
Unless a child learns otherwise, the sameness of all sorts of people is more apparent than the differences.

The child's point of view is also clearly represented by the Yook
grandson in the book, who is being told a saga by his grandfather.
The boy disappears after the first seven pages, but the opening of
the story, set in a time "On the last day of summer, / ten hours
before fall . . . ," suggests the beginning of school, or at least the
end of something quite pleasurable. The boy's anxiety is clear
from his grandfather's dragging him to the wall, where the grandfather begins narrating the story, telling of the differences between Yooks and Zooks, and the escalation of problems between
the two nations. The boy disappears while the grandfather remin-
isces. At the end of the book, just as the grandfather is proceeding
out to the wall with the Boomeroo, the boy reappears.

Though the grandfather chastises him for not being in the
bunker with the other Yooks, he does make clear that the boy has
a role at this time. "You will see me make history! / RIGHT
HERE! AND RIGHT NOW!" The boy will be a historian, if he
lives, marking this most important event in history. He shimmies
up a tree to watch the confrontation of Yook and Zook, and calls
out, "Grandpa! . . . Be Careful! Oh, gee!" The grandfather's responsibility in exposing his grandson to peril is clear to the reader
if not to grandfather or grandson. But the grandfather bears the
responsibility nonetheless. The final page is a child's indictment
of adults for letting matters come to such an impasse. And though
children may have a role in resolving the impasse, and certainly
will be involved later in their lives (if events allow them to reach
adulthood), it is still the actions of the adults that are clearly at
issue here.

The grandfather's counsel to "Be patient. . . . We'll see" only
prolongs the tension that has been mounting throughout the
book. Patience is not a virtue of children, nor is toleration of tension. The tension is something of a motivator here; it must be
resolved. But the delicate balance of Boomeroos poised to be
dropped cannot be resolved by action, but by inaction, albeit ac-

companied by negotiation. So the call is both to action and to inaction, a difficult point for children to understand, but one that is clearly well embodied in the book.

The book is not without its problems, particularly in the framing device of the reminiscence of the grandfather Yook being told to his grandson. The story opens as though the first events took place long ago, in the grandfather's youth. The escalation of arms occurs rapidly, without the sense of a considerable passage of time. But at the end, the grandfather and grandson are reunited at the wall, as if they had somehow left it, and as if the events of the reminiscence are going on in the present. Though the incongruity of time patterns may have a literary point—the events are not long past, but are important now—overall, it seems as if the device of the frame tale has simply fallen apart. There is some sense of time passing in the story, since the grandfather starts out remembering himself looking quite young, and ages and tires in appearance as the story progresses. But the imminent war seems part of the reminiscence, and not something likely to involve the grandson in his own lifetime.

The parallels to historical events are manifest throughout, starting with the wall, which seems like the Berlin Wall, dividing two peoples who are essentially alike, although it looks more like the Great Wall of China, which gives it a sense of historical longevity. The grandfather sent out to drop the Boomeroo seems to have his place in history, just like Paul Tibbetts dropping the first atomic bomb on Hiroshima. Even the slogans of the Yooks—"Keep Your Butter Side Up" and "Fight for the Butter Side Up! . . . Do or die!," since butter side up is "the right honest way!"—all ring true to American sentiments and American slogans. Even the march of all the Yooks into the fallout shelter, with supreme confidence in their leader and assurance that there will be a life to come back to after the Boomeroo, reminds the older reader of the fallout shelter building of the 1950s and 1960s, and of the later debates about whether nuclear war is winnable or survivable.

The confidence of grandfather in the "Boys in the Back Room" and in their technology is a particularly damning critique of American faith in advanced weaponry. The grandfather's feeling of confidence is a result of the new weapons he is provided and the grander, more foppish uniforms he wears to bolster his confidence each time he engages in a new confrontation with the enemy Zook. But this archrival, always the same Zook, is named Van Itch. Though the name is foreign sounding, of unspecific origin to American ears, it is also suggestive of the kind of threat posed by this Zook, for he is no more dangerous or annoying than an itch, an irritation that should be tolerated rather than threatened within an inch of mutually assured self-destruction.

But the Yook grandfather is not totally responsible for the escalation. The chief Yookeroo keeps assuaging the grandfather's sense of failure at every confrontation and prods him into new confrontations with excuses, uniforms, and weaponry; though the reader may suppose that if the Yook grandfather refused to carry on the confrontations, another Yook would take his place. The more invidious threat is the sentiment of the general Yook population. It is they who taunt the Yook when he fails, who form a marching band and a cheerleader squad of "Right-Side-Up Song Girls," and who make the issue more than just a border skirmish of two creatures. They invoke issues of honor in their song, "Oh, be faithful! / Believe in thy butter!" They make the issue one of battle and of life or death with their chant, "Fight for the Butter Side Up! / Do or die!" rather than just leaving the confrontation on the level of scare tactics. Had they not followed the instruction of the chief Yookeroo to retreat into the fallout shelter, it is not clear whether the ultimate confrontation would have taken place. If only the Yook grandfather and Van Itch had been left alone to patrol the border armed with slingshots and stickle-bush whips, the issue might have remained isolated and might have been forgotten. But with the interest of the entire Yook populace, the quality of the rhetoric and the weaponry escalates to extremes.

Though the book is a controversial one, it has sold well and has been well received in many quarters because it dares to confront an issue that many adults do not know how to introduce to children. But children, even young ones, are not nearly so naive that they do not know about bombs and the possibility of world annihilation. The book calls on children to abandon physical, confrontational methods of resolving conflicts, and to entertain the possibility of discussion and negotiation, even at the level of childhood arguments. But more important, it calls on adults to question why the situation has become as dire as it has, and to resolve it, on behalf of the world's children. Seuss admits that the book is not necessarily one exclusively for children, but by giving children a book on such an important, though admittedly terrifying, subject, he grants dignity to children's understanding and their ability to handle such matters, possibly in a more sensible way than their elders have.

You're Only Old Once!

Dr. Seuss's latest book is one which frankly admits its intention to appeal to adults. *You're Only Old Once!* is subtitled *A Book for Obsolete Children.* It is also the only Seuss book published by Random House with a dust jacket over a pictureless cover. Even the back of the dustcover suggests to the unwary buyer that this is not a book for children.

> Is this a children's book?
> Well . . . not immediately.
> You buy a copy for your child now
> and you give it to him on his 70th birthday.[12]

The text is not consistently in rhyme, and the back cover features two unpleasantly looking doctors, white jackets and stethescopes clearly displayed, glaring out of the doors of their offices. The front cover is not inviting to the reader, since there are more doctors there, albeit without such fierce looks. Clearly, these are not the tactics of the specialist on getting children to read and to enjoy books.

The book's date of publication was 2 March 1986, Dr. Seuss's eighty-second birthday. It is dedicated to the remaining classmates of Dr. Seuss's from the class of 1925 at Dartmouth. These reminders of the author's age, and the book's title, prepare the reader for an investigation into the issues surrounding old age, especially the way that the medical profession deals with old people's physical complaints. Though lighthearted and comical, the book's main point is a critique of the medical profession and the costly, irrelevant, rude, and sometimes pointless treatments given to patients. The book takes potshots at medical specialties, tests, prescriptions, and billing procedures, all of which the author had recently submitted to during a bout of serious illness. It satirizes nearly everything that happens to a patient once he submits himself and his pocketbook to the medical profession.

The book's central character, who undergoes all the medical procedures, is not named, nor does he do anything but submit to the rigors of the clinic and clinicians. He is simply the occasion for all the procedures, and not a real actor in the book. There is nothing seriously wrong with him. As the book says at the end, "you're in pretty good shape / for the shape you are in." So the ending is upbeat, and the criticisms not likely to offend anyone or reform the medical system. Though the book is certainly not a brilliant one, it is still enjoyable, especially because its humor is so prevalent.

6

The Cat's Place in History

Clearly Dr. Seuss's influence has been most felt on the industry producing beginner reading books. In fact, his Beginner Book division of Random House inspired a number of other publishing houses to start lines of beginner reading books modeled after *The Cat in the Hat*. A number of authors who might not otherwise have broken into print found the way open for them. For writers such as Arnold Lobel, who claim to possess the ideal easy-reader mentality and for whom the confines of the limited vocabulary have posed no problem in the creation of interesting stories, there was now a market. Lobel has taken Seuss's example even further by developing an interesting character into a whole series of books, each containing several short stories of limited vocabulary, about Frog and Toad. Mercer Mayer has taken the limited vocabulary one step further in his wordless picture books and his nearly wordless contributions to the "Look Look" series of Golden Books for beginning readers. Jan and Stan Berenstain have created their bears and spun the story line into several volumes as well. Richard Scarry has created many different kinds of books, including large dictionaries for children. Unlike the Beginner Books and Bright and Early books of Random House, several of these series are now issued in paperback and marketed even more cheaply than the Random House books. But had Dr. Seuss and Random House not begun marketing their books the way they did, the supply of inexpensive books for children would have been limited to these inexpensive series, some of whose titles are of dubious quality.

Dr. Seuss has also left his mark on the textbook publishing industry. Basal readers are still published. But with alternatives such as *The Cat in the Hat* and the other Beginner Books for children, textbook publishers have clearly felt the pressure to produce more interesting stories in their basal readers, and better artwork to accompany those stories. Though no basal reader has yet achieved popular book status among child readers, the use of controlled word lists has been relaxed and children now have supplementary reading material, which dignifies the reading experience by showing them the pleasure and the interest that more experienced readers feel in the process.

Seuss had also consistently challenged the limits of the conventions of children's literature. His famous Cat is a bad one, naughty and playful, and delightful for just those reasons. *On beyond Zebra!* goes so far as to mock traditional school lessons. What happens in his stories clearly would not receive approval from those adults who feel that literature should teach proper conduct by holding forth only positive examples. But it is hard to take the optimistic, personable Cat's transgressions too seriously, especially since nothing truly bad ever happens in the story. Even his worst actions can be repaired and rescued. And it is difficult to take his fantasies, even when they verge on parody, in any way other than lightheartedly, as they were intended. Seuss books are fun, and though some teach morals, most are just content to observe the world and invite the child reader to have fun living life.

The other challenge that Seuss has offered to children's literature is most apparent in his "message" books late in his career, *The Lorax* and *The Butter Battle Book*. His purpose in each of those books has been to challenge readers of all ages, including younger ones, to action, in order to resolve dire threats to life as we know it. His confrontation of the issue of nuclear war in *The Butter Battle Book* is the most shocking, since it confronts universal death, an issue that offends the sensibilities of most adults so deeply that it is commonly thought an inappropriate issue to present to children. But as in *The Lorax,* Dr. Seuss does not ask simply that children contemplate the issue, thereby torturing themselves with unthinkable thoughts. He calls for action and enables the child reader to do something. In *The Lorax,* children are taught about the frivolity of some consumer goods and the positive harm of buying those goods if their manufacture damages the ecosystem. As part of the solution, children are given the option of cultivating living things and protecting them so that they can flourish. In *The Butter Battle Book,* the argument between the Yooks and the Zooks is so extreme that most children can be led to see that discussion, negotiation, and peaceful coexistence are all options, and that even uncomfortable coexistence is preferable to mutually assured self-destruction. Dr. Seuss is not simply trying to make children aware of these important issues; he is also positing models for children to follow. He wants to empower children, rather than drive them to despair. He also implies that children are smart enough to understand these issues; they need not be helpless victims.

In fact, empowering children and encouraging mastery and independence is one of the central themes in all of Dr. Seuss's works for children. In the Beginner Books, Seuss encourages children to read by themselves. He gives all manner of clues in the text and in the illustration to move the reader on to understanding and to the end of the story. Even reluctant readers are encouraged by visual clues in the pictures and by orthographic conventions that make the reading easier. Furthermore, Seuss makes the process a pleasant one, rewarding the effort it takes to get through the text. Though his Beginner Books and Bright and Early books can be read out loud, for the most part they succeed better with silent reading. The rewards to the solo child reader the first time he actually reads such a book are difficult to quantify, but the qualities that result can only be positive. The child has learned a mature skill and is rewarded for his competence with an interesting story. By recording stories like those children tell themselves, Seuss gives dignity to those fantasies and demonstrates the power of the mind even when it is young.

Elsewhere, Seuss's message about the power of the human

mind to create interesting and marvelous thoughts is clear. *Hunches in Bunches* catalogs a child's thought processes while considering solutions to a problem. The ingenious possibilities are delightful and interesting. As the narrator says in *One Fish, Two Fish,*

> From there to here,
> from here to there,
> funny things
> are everywhere.[1]

The challenge is to see the possibilities of funniness by closely observing the world. Throughout his books, Seuss both challenges the child reader to be creative and imaginative, and suggests ways to look at the world that are entertaining and active, clear antidotes to boredom. Once again, he empowers the child to entertain himself, praising the child's own inner resources and creativity. Seuss's propensity to create a tall tale, one which strives to be the best, rewards children's desire to be extraordinary. Once again, ordinary children are encouraged to stretch their skills by Seuss's example.

Dr. Seuss books also build positive self-images in children. The titles of some of his lesser-known works make clear the messages of the books: *I Can Write—By Me, Myself* and *I Can Draw It Myself* have half-titles "with some help from Dr. Seuss." Though the child needs help, a least initially, in writing and drawing, by the end of these workbooks the child can demonstrate the same abilities that Dr. Seuss has as an author and illustrator. In fact, by the end of each book, the child is an author and illustrator. Dr. Seuss's simple language and cartoonlike illustrations, with thick definite lines and monotone, unshaded primary colors, are all childlike, similar to the writing and drawing that children produce. By making the task look simple, Seuss encourages children to try their own skills at doing what he does.

The Shape of Me and *My Book about Myself* are the two most representative titles of this emphasis on the child reader's positive self-image. Each invites the child to notice differences in people and to celebrate those differences, especially those differences in himself. The books ask the reader to look carefully in order to see those differences. In fact, in spite of his fantastic flights, Dr. Seuss's main message about how to be interesting, both to oneself and to others, is to observe reality carefully. By playing with the realistic, by use of opposites and comparisons, one can see life's possibilities, funny and otherwise. Being interesting to oneself is the prime goal in life; that quality mastered, everything else interesting flows from it.

This emphasis on and glorification of individuality is a particularly American trait, like many others celebrated in Dr. Seuss. In his books, life is always new and fascinating. Even the most mundane objects become fascinating when carefully observed. Fun is in the eye of the beholder and the original thinker. Life and individuals are all good and all held up for admiration in Dr. Seuss. And yet his characters are not superheroes. In fact, many, like Bartholomew, Horton, Thidwick, the grandfather Yook, and even the Cat, are ordinary, at least until extraordinary circumstances call forth extraordinary behavior from them. Their ability to rise to the occasion makes them exceptional, but after their stories are over, they sink back into obscurity. Individuality and heroism, then, reside in ordinary people. One should celebrate those virtues even when not necessarily called upon to exercise them. These virtues—loyalty, perseverance, hospitality, truthfulness—are extraordinary in these characters only because of the lengths to which they go to be consistent in practicing them. But they are all-American traits, which most American children can practice. So they can choose to emulate Seuss's heroic characters themselves.

It is in his choice of his heroes that Dr. Seuss shows his clearest link to Frank Capra, but Seuss's film experience has had an even wider, more profound influence on the author. From his filmmaking experience, Dr. Seuss gained a sense of what makes an interesting story—fast pacing, minor cliff-hangers within the story to lure the reader on, visual clues to help the reader interpret the story, shortened length in order not to tax the reader's sometimes limited attention span. From film he learned the importance of an interesting opening and a satisfying closing. Some of Dr. Seuss's endings, especially in *How the Grinch Stole Christmas!* and *Horton Hears a Who!* show some difficulty in arriving at a satisfactory denouement, and perhaps reveal the author's difficulty in finding an adequate ending to the story. Therefore, some of Dr. Seuss's stories end abruptly. But the endings are no less satisfying or apt for their brevity; the stories almost always end with no loose ends straggling on behind, except in the later "message" books, where part of the message is the open ending.

Dr. Seuss's understanding of film also helped him adapt some of his books to full-length animated features for television. Clearly, his knowledge of both television and film guided his artistic control of these adaptations, and their success lay in his high standards of production and the faithfulness of the adaptations to the originals, without being slavishly loyal to the books. The Academy Awards of his early career were clearly not misplaced, as witnessed by the later awards his television specials have won for him. Of course, the television specials have also helped maintain popular interest in his books at the same time.

Of all the influences most directly observable on Seuss's illustration, his experience in drawing cartoons in college deserves special mention. The single panel containing both text and picture, and the limited number of panels for each comic strip, forced an economy of language and illustration, which would serve the author well in his writing for children. At the same time, the artwork could be less than great art, as long as it was expressive. In the cartoon strip, artwork needs to carry the message beyond what the language can do. Seuss's understanding of the cartoon strip dynamic is one of the most popularizing of his techniques. To tell a story in miniature, with emphasis on the visual, is perfect preparatory experience for writing an interesting book for the very young, one that will capture and hold their interest, while at the same time encouraging them to read.

Seuss's awareness of the commercial possibilities for his books deserves particular comment as well. Though he has broken much new ground in the field of children's literature, he has not suffered unpopularity because of his originality. Not only are his works particularly American in theme, he has also had a sure sense of what the American market for children's books would buy. The marketing of the books has been particularly astute, guided not only by his editors, but also by Seuss himself as president of the Beginner Books division of Random House. Even as early as *Mulberry Street* Seuss understood Americans' desire for fantasy for their children, and the combination of the learning-to-read angle with the fantasy in *The Cat in the Hat* was not only inspired, it was shrewd. The translation of the Beginner Books into foreign languages, though not particularly successful (since the poetry does not translate well), shows Seuss's sense of markets to be reached with his books, even if the books are somewhat compromised by their transmutation in order to suit the needs of the new market. The meteoric sales of his books have not been mere strokes of luck, but the result of careful, if not always conscious, calculation.

One of the traits that Dr. Seuss seems to have intuited about his original audience for *The Cat in the Hat* is the propensity of baby boomers to break rules, to re-create institutions in forms more to their own liking than the originals. In *The Cat,* Seuss gave the child reader a model of a beginner book that broke the bland conventions of a basal reader by telling an outrageous story through the use of sometimes outrageous language. Though Dr. Spock's permissive discipline for children has frequently been credited with spurring the youthful rebellion of the 1960s, Dr. Seuss might equally be given credit, since he demonstrates a kind of permissiveness with language: almost any use of it is sanctioned as long as it amuses.

By bringing interesting reading materials to children, Seuss gave a new dignity and interest to the field of children's literature. Simply because his books are not high literature, and appear deceptively simple in both language and illustration, does not mean that there is no literary or artistic value to them or that they are effortless productions dashed off in a weekend. By putting such effort into his books, Seuss dignifies child readers and reading, giving them extraordinary efforts and excellent products. His massive popularity does not imply a crass diminution of his art. Being popular does not mean being second-rate.

More than anything else, Dr. Seuss's books have brought pleasure to both children and adults. The citations for many of his honors have singled out this one accomplishment above all others. Life is good and to be enjoyed. Life is also funny and to be laughed at. Most of his inventions of language are aimed more at pleasing than at anything else. For all that he has been cited as a moralistic writer, his main goal is to entertain with a good story. In this goal he has succeeded admirably.

Notes and References

Chapter 1

1. Herbert Kupferberg, "A Seussian Celebration," *Parade Magazine,* 26 February 1984, 5.
2. Rob Wilder, "Catching Up with Dr. Seuss," *Parents Magazine,* June 1979, 62.
3. *If I Ran the Circus* (New York: Random House, 1956), n. p.
4. Marian Christy, "A Muse on the Loose," *Boston Globe,* 20 July 1980, sec. C, 4.
5. Ibid., sec. C, 4.
6. Wilder, "Catching Up," 62.
7. "Malice in Wonderland," *Newsweek,* 9 February 1942, 58.
8. Wilder, "Catching Up," 64.
9. Carolyn See, "Dr. Seuss and the Naked Ladies," *Esquire,* June 1974, 119.
10. Christy, "Muse," sec. C, 4.
11. Ibid., sec. C, 1.
12. Richard Marschall, ed., *The Tough Coughs as He Ploughs the Dough* (New York: William Morrow, 1986).
13. Ibid., 12.
14. Kathy Hacker, "Happy 80th Birthday, Dr. Seuss!" *Philadelphia Inquirer,* 7 March 1984, sec. E, 3.
15. "Children's Book Best Sellers, 1895–1975," from *80 Years of Best Sellers, 1895–1975* (New York: Xerox, 1977), cited in Alan C. Purves and Dianne L. Monson, *Experiencing Children's Literature* (Glenview, Ill.: Scott, Foresman, 1984), 32.
16. Jennifer Crichton, "Dr. Seuss Turns 80," *Publishers Weekly,* 10 February 1984, 23.
17. Kupferberg, "Seussian Celebration," 5.
18. Karla Kushkin, "Seuss at 75," *New York Times Book Review,* 29 April 1979, 42.

Chapter 2

1. *And To Think That I Saw It on Mulberry Street* (New York: Vanguard, 1937), n.p.; hereafter cited in the text.

2. Clifton Fadiman, "Children's Literature Then and Now: From Kenneth Grahame's *Wind in the Willows* to Dr. Seuss's *Cat in the Hat*," *Holiday,* April 1959, 16.

3. Michael Steig, "Dr. Seuss's Attack on Imagination: *I Wish That I Had Duck Feet* and the Cautionary Tale," in *Proceedings of the Ninth Annual Conference of the Children's Literature Association, University of Florida, March 1982,* ed. Priscilla A. Ord (The Children's Literature Association, 1983), 137–41.

4. *The Five Hundred Hats of Bartholomew Cubbins* (New York: Vanguard, 1938), n.p.; hereafter cited in the text.

5. Jill P. May, "Dr. Seuss and *The 500 Hats of Bartholomew Cubbins*," *CLA Bulletin* 9, no. 3 (1985): 8–9.

6. *Horton Hatches the Egg* (New York: Random House, 1940), n.p.; hereafter cited in the text.

Chapter 3

1. *McElligot's Pool* (New York: Random House, 1947), n.p.; hereafter cited in the text.

2. Lorrene Love Ort, "Theodore Seuss Geisel—The Children's Dr. Seuss," *Elementary English,* 32 (1955): 136.

3. Wilder, "Catching Up," 63.

4. *Thidwick, the Big-Hearted Moose* (New York: Random House, 1948), n.p.; hereafter cited in the text.

5. *Bartholomew and the Oobleck* (New York: Random House, 1949), n.p.; hereafter cited in the text.

6. *If I Ran the Zoo* (New York: Random House, 1950), n.p.; hereafter cited in the text.

7. *If I Ran the Circus* (New York: Random House, 1950), n.p.; hereafter cited in the text.

8. *Horton Hears a Who!* (New York: Random House, 1954), n.p.; hereafter cited in the text.

9. David Sheff, "Seuss on Wry," *Parenting Magazine,* February 1987, 55.

10. *On Beyond Zebra!* (New York: Random House, 1955), n.p.; hereafter cited in the text.

11. Barbara Bader, *American Picturebooks: From Noah's Ark to the Beast Within* (New York: Macmillan, 1976; London: Collier, 1976), 309.

12. Cynthia Gorney, "Grinch, Hippo-heimer, Cat in Hat, Wocket, He's Got Generations of Kids in His Pocket," *Washington Post,* 21 May 1979, B3.

13. *How the Grinch Stole Christmas!* (New York: Random House, 1958), n.p.; hereafter cited in the text.

14. Sheff, "Seuss on Wry," 56.

Chapter 4

1. *The Cat in the Hat* (New York: Random House, 1957), n.p.; hereafter cited in the text.

2. John Hersey, "Why Do Students Bog Down on the First R? A Local Committee Sheds Light on a National Problem: Reading," *Life,* 24 May 1954, 148, ff.

3. Ibid., 148.

4. "My Hassle With First Grade Reading," *Education* 78 (1958): 324.

5. Myra Barrs, "Laughing Your Way to Literacy," *Times Educational Supplement,* 23 January 1976, 20.

6. Cited in Betsy Marden Silverman, "Dr. Seuss Talks to Parents about Learning to Read and What Makes Children Want to Do It," *Parents,* November 1960, 135.

7. Hersey, "Why Do Students," 136.

8. Mary Lystad, *From Dr. Mather to Dr. Seuss: 200 Years of American Books for Children* (Boston: G. K. Hall, 1980), 201.

9. Leonore Fleischer, "Authors and Editors," *Publishers Weekly,* 2 December 1968, 7.

10. Barrs, "Laughing," 20.

11. Don L. F. Nilsen, "Dr. Seuss as Grammar Consultant," *Language Arts* 54 (1977): 69.

12. *The Cat in the Hat Comes Back* (New York: Random House, 1958), n.p.; hereafter cited in the text.

13. Purves and Monson, *Experiencing Children's Literature,* 32.

14. *I Can Read with My Eyes Shut!* (New York: Random House, 1978), n.p.; hereafter cited in the text.

15. Fadiman, "Children's Literature," 16.

16. Theo. LeSieg, *Wacky Wednesday* (New York: Random House, 1974).

17. "Wacky World of Dr. Seuss," *Life,* 6 April 1959, 113.

18. Silverman, "Dr. Seuss Talks to Parents," 137.

19. Ibid.

20. Richard R. Lingeman, "Dr. Seuss, Theo. Le Sieg," *New York Times Book Review,* 14 November 1976, 48.

21. E. J. Kahn, "Profiles: Children's Friend," *New Yorker,* 17 December 1960, 92.

22. Fleischer, "Authors and Editors," 7.

23. Bruno Bettelheim, *On Learning to Read: Children's Fascination with Language* (New York: Knopf, 1982), 10–12 ff.

24. LeSieg, *Wacky Wednesday,* flyleaf.

25. John Gough, "The Unsung Dr. Seuss: Theo. LeSieg," *Children's Literature Association Quarterly* 11 (Winter 1986–87): 185.

26. Lingeman, "Theo. LeSieg," 24.

27. Gough, "Unsung Dr. Seuss," 184.

28. Fadiman, "Children's Literature," 17.

29. Purves and Monson, *Experiencing Children's Literature,* 32.

30. *Green Eggs and Ham* (New York: Random House, 1960), n.p.; hereafter cited in the text.

31. Purves and Monson, *Experiencing Children's Literature,* 31.

32. Ibid.

33. Ibid.

Chapter 5

1. John P. Bailey, Jr., "Three Decades of Dr. Seuss," *Elementary English* 42 (1965): 11.

2. Jeff Lyon, "Writing for Adults, It Seems, Is One of Dr. Seuss's Dreams," *Chicago Tribune,* 15 April 1982, sec. 3, 10.

3. *The Lorax* (New York: Random House, 1971), n.p.; hereafter cited in the text.

4. *The Butter Battle Book* (New York: Random House, 1984), n.p.; hereafter cited in the text.

5. "Most Kids Say Yooks Should Talk to Zooks," *USA Today,* 29 June 1984: 11A.

6. Nancy Carlsson-Paige and Diane E. Levin, *"The Butter Battle Book;* Uses and Abuses with young Children," *Young Children* 41 (1986): 41.

7. Carlsson-Paige and Levin, "Butter Battle," 38.

8. Daniel R. Bechtel, "Dr. Seuss, Prophet to Giant-Killers," *Christian Century,* 11 April 1984, 359.

9. John Garvey, "Guns and Butter; Dr. Seuss's Liberal Sentimentality," *Commonweal,* 10 August 1984, 423–24.

10. *National Review,* 27 July 1984, 15.

11. Crichton, "Dr. Seuss Turns 80," 23.

12. *You're Only Old Once!* (New York: Random House, 1986).

Chapter 6

1. *One Fish, Two Fish, Red Fish, Blue Fish* (New York: Random House, 1960), n.p.

Selected Bibliography

Primary Sources

1. Books for Children (Nonseries)

And To Think That I Saw It on Mulberry Street. New York: Vanguard, 1937; London: Country Life, 1939.

Bartholomew and the Oobleck. New York: Random House, 1949.

The Butter Battle Book. New York: Random House, 1984.

The Cat in the Hat Dictionary, by the Cat Himself. With Philip D. Eastman. New York: Random House, 1964.

The Cat in the Hat Songbook. New York: Random House, 1967.

Did I Ever Tell You How Lucky You Are? New York: Random House, 1973; London: Collins, 1974.

Dr. Seuss's Sleep Book. New York: Random House, 1962; London: Collins, 1964.

The Five Hundred Hats of Bartholomew Cubbins. New York: Vanguard, 1938; London: Oxford University Press, 1940.

Happy Birthday to You! New York: Random House, 1959.

Horton Hatches the Egg. New York: Random House, 1940; London: Hamish Hamilton, 1942.

Horton Hears a Who! New York: Random House, 1954; London: Collins, 1976.

How the Grinch Stole Christmas! New York: Random House, 1957.

Hunches in Bunches. New York: Random House, 1982.

I Can Lick 30 Tigers Today and Other Stories. New York: Random House, 1969; London: Collins, 1970.

I Had Trouble in Getting to Solla Sollew. New York: Random House, 1965; London: Collins, 1967.

If I Ran the Circus. New York: Random House, 1956; London: Collins, 1969.

If I Ran the Zoo. New York: Random House, 1950.

The King's Stilts. New York: Random House, 1939; London: Hamish Hamilton, 1942.

The Lorax. New York: Random House, 1971; London: Collins, 1972.

McElligot's Pool. New York: Random House, 1947; London: Collins, 1975.

On beyond Zebra! New York: Random House, 1955.

Scrambled Eggs Super! New York: Random House, 1953.

The Sneetches and Other Stories. New York: Random House, 1961; London: Collins, 1965.

Thidwick, the Big-Hearted Moose. New York: Random House, 1948; London: Collins, 1968.

Yertle the Turtle and Other Stories. New York: Random House, 1958; London: Collins, 1963.

2. Beginner Books

[Rosetta Stone, pseud.] *Because a Little Bug Went Ka-Choo!* Illustrated by Michael Frith. New York: Random House, 1975.

The Cat in the Hat. New York: Houghton Mifflin, Random House, 1957; London: Hutchinson, 1958.

The Cat in the Hat Comes Back. New York: Random House, 1958; London: Collins, 1961.

The Cat's Quizzer. New York: Random House, 1976; London: Collins, 1977.

[Theo. LeSieg, pseud.] *Come Over to My House.* Illustrated by Richard Erdoes. New York: Random House, 1966; London: Collins, 1967.

Dr. Seuss's ABC. New York: Random House, 1963; London: Collins, 1964.

Fox in Socks. New York: Random House, 1965; London: Collins, 1966.

Green Eggs and Ham. New York: Random House, 1960; London: Collins, 1962.

[Theo. LeSieg, pseud.] *Hooper Humperdink. . . ? Not Him!* Illustrated by Charles Martin. New York: Random House, 1976; London: Collins, 1977.

Hop on Pop. New York: Random House, 1963; London: Collins, 1964.

I Am Not Going to Get Up Today!. Illustrated by James Stevenson. New York: Random House, 1987.

I Can Draw It Myself. New York: Random House, 1970.

I Can Read with My Eyes Shut! New York: Random House, 1978.

[Theo. LeSieg, pseud.] *I Wish That I Had Duck Feet.* Illustrated by B. Tobey. New York: Random House, 1965; London: Collins, 1967.

[Theo. LeSieg, pseud.] *Maybe You Should Fly a Jet! Maybe You Should Be a Vet!.* Illustrated by Michael Smollin. New York: Random House, 1980; London: Collins, 1981.

My Book about Me—By Me, Myself. I Wrote It! I Drew It! Illustrated by Roy McKie. New York: Random House, 1969.

Oh Say Can You Say? New York: Random House, 1979; London: Collins, 1980.

Oh, the Thinks You Can Think! New York: Random House, 1975; London: Collins, 1976.

One Fish, Two Fish, Red Fish, Blue Fish. New York: Random House, 1960; London: Collins, 1962.

[Theo. LeSieg, pseud.] *Please Try to Remember the First of Octember.* Illustrated by Arthur Cummings. New York: Random House, 1977; London: Collins, 1978.

[Theo. LeSieg, pseud.] *Ten Apples up on Top!* Illustrated by Roy McKie. New York: Random House, 1961; London: Collins, 1963.

[Theo. LeSieg, pseud.] *Wacky Wednesday.* Illustrated by George Booth. New York: Random House, 1974; London: Collins, 1975.

3. Bright and Early Books

[Theo. LeSieg, pseud.] *The Eye Book.* Illustrated by Roy McKie. New York: Random House, 1968; London: Collins, 1969.

The Foot Book. New York: Random House, 1968; London: Collins, 1969.

Great Day for Up! Illustrated by Quentin Blake. New York: Random House, 1974; London: Collins, 1975.

[Theo. LeSieg, pseud.] *I Can Write—By Me, Myself.* New York: Random House, 1971.

[Theo. LeSieg, pseud.] *In a People House.* Illustrated by Roy McKie. New York: Random House, 1972; London: Collins, 1973.

[Theo. LeSieg, pseud.] *The Many Mice of Mr. Brice.* Illustrated by Roy McKie. New York: Random House, 1973; London: Collins, 1974.

Marvin K. Mooney, Will You Please Go Now? New York: Random House, 1972; London: Collins, 1973.

Mr. Brown Can Moo! Can You? New York: Random House, 1970; London: Collins, 1971.

The Shape of Me and Other Stuff. New York: Random House, 1973; London: Collins, 1974.

There's a Wocket in My Pocket! New York: Random House, 1974; London: Collins, 1975.

[Theo. LeSieg, pseud.] *The Tooth Book.* Illustrated by Roy McKie. New York: Random House, 1981.

[Theo. LeSieg, pseud.] *Would You Rather Be a Bullfrog?* Illustrated by Roy McKie. New York: Random House, 1975; London: Collins, 1976.

4. Adult Books

Boners. Illustrated by Dr. Seuss. New York: Viking, 1930.

Dr. Seuss from Then to Now: A Catalogue of the Retrospective Exhibition. San Diego: San Diego Museum of Art, 1986.

More Boners. Illustrated by Dr. Seuss. New York: Viking, 1931.

The Seven Lady Godivas. New York: Random House, 1939; rpt. 1987.

The Tough Coughs as He Ploughs the Dough: Early Writings and Cartoons by Dr. Seuss. Edited by Richard Marschall. New York: Morrow, Remco Worldservice Books, 1987.

You're Only Old Once! New York: Random House, 1986.

Secondary Sources

Bailey, John P., Jr. "Three Decades of Dr. Seuss." *Elementary English* 42 (1965): 7–12. An overview of Dr. Seuss's writing and an evaluation of his progression through his career.

Bandler, Michael J. "For Kids over the Age of 70." *Newsday*, 3 March 1986, Pt. 2, 4–5. A review of *You're Only Old Once!* along with a report about Seuss's current activities.

———. "Seuss on the Loose." *Parents*, September 1987, 116–120 ff. A retrospective of the author's career.

Barrs, Myra. "Laughing Your Way to Literacy." *Times Educational Supplement*, 23 January 1976, 20–21. An examination of Dr. Seuss's American appeal, his design in plotting, and his use of language.

Burns, Thomas A. "Dr. Seuss' *How the Grinch Stole Christmas:* Its Recent Acceptance into the American Popular Christmas Tradition." *New York Folklore* 2 (1976): 191–204. Examines reasons for popular acceptance of *Grinch*.

Chambers, Aidan. "Idiosyncratic Originality." *Times Educational Supplement*, 11 February 1973, 43. An assessment of Seuss's use of narrative and his ability to write simply.

Cott, Jonathan. "The Good Dr. Seuss." In *Pipers at the Gates of Dawn: The Wisdom of Children's Literature*, 1–37. New York: Random House, 1983. Examines the qualities which are new to children's books which Dr. Seuss introduced.

Christy, Marian. "A Muse on the Loose." *Boston Globe*, 20 July 1980, sec. C, 1, 5. Reporting on Dr. Seuss's themes throughout his career.

Conklin, Ellis E. "Dr. Seuss: Doing In Dick and Jane." Martinsburg, West

Virginia *Evening Journal,* 13 September 1986, 8–9. Summarizes Seuss's improvements in the early-reader genre.

Crichton, Jennifer. "Dr. Seuss Turns 80." *Publishers Weekly,* 10 February 1984, 22–23. Reporting Seuss's purpose in writing *The Butter Battle Book.*

Dohm, Janice H. "The Curious Case of Dr. Seuss: A Minority Report from America." *Junior Bookshelf* 27 (1963): 323–29. A British perspective on Seuss, helping to identify his particular appeal to Americans.

Fadiman, Clifton. "Children's Literature Then and Now: From Kenneth Grahame's *Wind in the Willows* to Dr. Seuss's *Cat in the Hat.*" *Holiday* 25 (1959): 11, 14–17. Particular focus on *Mulberry Street* and the circumstances of its publication; comments particularly on the lack of personal information found in Seuss's books.

Fleischer, Leonore. "Authors and Editors." *Publishers Weekly* 2 December 1968, 7–8. Records Seuss's philosophy behind the Bright and Early series.

Gorney, Cynthia. "Grinch, Hippo-heimer, Cat in Hat, Wocket, He's Got Generations of Kids in His Pocket." *Washington Post,* 21 May 1979, sec. B, 1, 3. Anecdotal material about "Yertle the Turtle," *Five Hundred Hats,* and Seuss's techniques in coloring his illustrations.

Gough, John. "The Unsung Dr. Seuss: Theo. LeSieg." *Children's Literature Association Quarterly* 11 (1986–87): 183–86. Discusses prevalent themes in the LeSieg books.

Greenleaf, Warren T. "How the Grinch Stole Reading: The Serious Nonsense of Dr. Seuss." *Principal* 61 (1982): 6–9. An assessment of Dr. Seuss's popularity with both children and adults.

Hersey, John. "Why Do Students Bog Down on the First *R?* A Local Committee Sheds Light on a National Problem: Reading." *Life,* 24 May 1954, 136–50. The article that first encouraged Seuss to write a beginning reader.

Hopkins, Lee Bennett. "Mother Goose's Sons and Daughters." *Teacher* 95 (1978): 36–38. Anecdotal material about Seuss's manner of composing a beginning reader.

Kahn, E. J., Jr. "Profiles: Children's Friend." *New Yorker,* 17 December 1960, 47 ff. Most thorough collection of biographical data on Seuss.

Kupferberg, Herbert. "A Seussian Celebration." *Parade Magazine,* 26 February 1984, 4–6. Biographical information, Seuss's attitude toward juvenile audiences.

Kushkin, Karla. "Seuss at 75." *New York Times Book Review,* 29 April 1979, 23, 42. Identifies the distinctive characteristics of Seuss's illustrations; notes Rosetta Stone as one of Seuss's pseudonyms.

Lingeman, Richard R. "Dr. Seuss, Theo. LeSieg." *New York Times Book*

Review, 14 November 1976, 24, 48. Identifies the difference between LeSieg's books and Seuss's.

Lyon, Jeff. "Writing for Adults, It Seems, Is One of Dr. Seuss' Dreams." *Chicago Tribune,* 15 April 1982, sec. 3, 1, 10. Reporting details of composition of *Hunches in Bunches; Grinch; You're Only Old Once!*

Lystad, Mary. *From Dr. Mather to Dr. Seuss: 200 Years of American Books for Children.* Boston: G. K. Hall, 1980. Places Dr. Seuss in the history of children's literature; particular commentary about his attitudes toward leisure and amusement.

"Malice in Wonderland." *Newsweek,* 9 February 1942, 58–59. Identifies Seuss's political cartoons during World War II, and the issues that led to their composition.

May, Jill P. "Dr. Seuss and *The 500 Hats of Bartholomew Cubbins.*" *CLA Bulletin* 9, no. 3 (1985): 8–9. Examines the appeal of the book, discusses teaching exercises using it.

Nilsen, Don L. F. "Dr. Seuss as Grammar Consultant." *Language Arts* 54 (1977): 567–71. Identifies the rhetorical devices that Seuss uses in his texts.

Ort, Lorene Love. "Theodore Seuss Geisel—The Children's Dr. Seuss." *Elementary English* 32 (1955): 135–42. Notes Seuss's appeals, both artistic and linguistic, to the beginner in reading.

Sale, Roger. *Fairy Tales and After: From Snow White to E. B. White.* Cambridge, Mass.: Harvard University Press, 1978, 8–12. A close examination of *Five Hundred Hats.*

Schroth, Evelyn. "Dr. Seuss and Language Use." *The Reading Teacher* 31 (1978): 748–50. Points out orthographical techniques that Seuss uses to make reading easier for young readers.

See, Carolyn. "Dr. Seuss and the Naked Ladies." *Esquire,* June 1974, 118–9, 176. Background material on the composition of *The Seven Lady Godivas.*

Sheff, David. "Seuss on Wry." *Parenting Magazine,* February 1987, 52–57. Examines Seuss's appeal both to children and to parents.

Silverman, Betsy Marden. "Dr. Seuss Talks to Parents; about Learning to Read and What Makes Children Want to Do It." *Parents,* November 1960, 44–45, 134–37. Attention particularly to the design behind Bright and Early and Beginner Books.

Steig, Michael. "Dr. Seuss's Attack on Imagination: *I Wish That I Had Duck Feet* and the Cautionary Tale." *Proceedings of the Ninth Annual Conference of the Children's Literature Association, University of Florida, March 1982.* Edited by Priscilla A. Ord (The Children's Literature Association, 1983), 137–41. Discusses Seuss's discouraging messages about the power and value of the imagination.

Sullivan, John. "Growing Up with Dr. Seuss." *American Baby,* August
    1984, 46, 52. A retrospective on the successes of various Dr. Seuss
    books.
Wilder, Rob. "Catching Up with Dr. Seuss." *Parents,* June 1979, 60–64.
    Anecdotal material about the circumstances of composition of vari-
    ous Seuss books.

Index

About the Author

Ruth K. MacDonald is professor of English at New Mexico State University, where she teaches literature for children. She received her B.A. and M.A. in English from the University of Connecticut, her Ph.D. in English from Rutgers University, and her M.B.A. from the University of Texas at El Paso. She is past president and treasurer of the Children's Literature Association and has chaired the divisions of children's literature for the Modern Language Association and the Northeast Modern Language Association. Her book *Literature for Children in England and America, 1646–1774* (Troy, N.Y.: Whitston Press, 1982) is a study of various genres of literature for children in the period. She has also contributed the Twayne United States Authors Series volume *Louisa May Alcott* and the Twayne English Authors Series volume *Beatrix Potter,* and is a field editor for Twayne.